AN
ENGLISHMAN'S
HOME

AN ENGLISHMAN'S HOME

Goodwood House, Broadlands, Arundel Castle,
Breamore House, Stratfield Saye, Penshurst Place, Wilton House,
Uppark, Sutton Place, Chartwell

John Miller

Countryside Books, Newbury
in association with TVS Television Ltd.

First Published 1985

© Text John Miller 1985

COUNTRYSIDE BOOKS
3 Catherine Road,
Newbury, Berkshire

ISBN 0 905392 46 9

Designed by Mon Mohan & Jo Angell

Photography by Tony Nutley

Produced through
MRM (Print Consultants) Ltd., Reading

Typesetting by Acorn Bookwork, Salisbury

Colour reproduction by
S&M Repro, Basingstoke

Colour plates printed by
Riverside Press (Reading)

Text printed and bound in England by
Woolnough Bookbinding, Wellingborough

CONTENTS

For Aileen

INTRODUCTION

'We shape our dwellings and afterwards our dwellings shape us.'
Winston Churchill

I came across this remark of Churchill's when I was researching the television series *An Englishman's Home*, and the truth of it kept coming back to me as I moved from one to another of the great houses we visited and talked to their present owners.

It was the Earl of March who first sowed the idea in my mind from which both this book and the television series subsequently grew. I had gone to see him at Goodwood about a completely different programme idea, and he casually asked whether I would like a quick tour of the house before lunch. Listening to his witty and often irreverent stories about his ancestors it dawned on me that if I could find another nine owners who could talk as well about their heritage as Lord March, we had the makings of a fascinating series.

The question that intrigued me was how was it possible to live a normal twentieth century life in a building that dated back several centuries. Most people would find the huge costs of upkeep and repair an intolerable burden. Pride in your family history loses some of its sheen if it is crumbling about your ears. All the owners of these ten houses have found their own solution to this dilemma, and speak frankly about how they reached it in the pages that follow. In selecting the houses for inclusion my criteria were two – that each should have an interesting story to tell, and the storyteller to do justice to it in words that would bring it alive. I tramped through several centuries of our history before finally settling on the ten that appear in this book.

When I was looking for an appropriate title my television presenter, Jill Cochrane, suggested *An Englishman's Home*. Most people know what they think is the second half of that quotation but, as so often when one checks back to the original source, it proved to be slightly different. It was coined by Chief Justice Coke in the second year of James I's reign, in his judgment on Semayne's Case: 'A man's house is his castle', or in another version: 'The home of every one is to him as his castle.'

But however noble the sentiments, one has to remember that even castles were not always inviolate. The only building in this book that still retains the title of Castle, Arundel, was sacked in the Civil War and only the Fitzalan

Chapel and the Keep survive from the earlier period. But nearly all of them have undergone changes down the centuries, as their family fortunes rose and fell. All of their owners have played their parts on the national stage, many of them have held the highest office, some died on the block or the battlefield, and some have changed the course of history. Their homes reflect a panorama of the past that still has lessons for the visitor today.

It was that great and perceptive historian Sir Lewis Namier who argued that 'English history, especially English Parliamentary history, is made by families rather than by individuals ... The English political family is a compound of "blood", name, and estate, this last, as the dominions of monarchs, being the most important of the three; that is why mansions instead of families are so often the object of monographs dealing with the history of the English upper classes'. Taken together, the history of these ten houses is a reflection through a glittering prism of many of the great and crucial events of the last five centuries.

The first owner of Penshurst Place financed Edward III's foreign wars. The first Howard Duke of Norfolk was created by Richard III, and his descendants served successive monarchs. Henry VIII gave Wilton to the Herbert family and Sutton Place to Sir Francis Weston. He also confiscated Penshurst from the Duke of Buckingham, but his son Edward VI gave it to the Sidney family and died in the arms of Henry Sidney. Elizabeth I gave Breamore to Sir Christopher Hatton and took counsel from the Sidneys and Dudleys. James I showered favours on two of the Herbert brothers. Charles I regularly visited Wilton, but the 4th Earl of Pembroke took Parliament's side in the Civil War. That terrible conflict divided the country and many of the families in these great houses too. Charles II sired the first Duke of Richmond who later bought Goodwood. The Hulses of Breamore came over with William of Orange in 1688 and served as physicians to George I and II. Many of these families fought in the Napoleonic Wars with the Duke of Wellington, and his descendants live in the house that the nation gave him at Stratfield Saye. The Prince Regent caroused with Sir Harry Fetherstonhaugh at Uppark. Edward VII and Elizabeth II have both held Privy Councils at Goodwood. Winston Churchill's home at Chartwell has now been presented to the nation in his memory.

On top of their historical significance all these houses are great treasure stores of priceless and beautiful pictures, furniture, sculpture, porcelain, and all manner of *objets d'art*, housed in some of the most spectacular architecture that has survived from earlier and grander days. Inigo Jones, Webb, Kent, 'Capability' Brown, Holland, Repton, Wyatt have all left their mark in earlier centuries, and in our own Sir Hugh Casson and Sir Geoffrey Jellicoe have wrought a modern Renaissance at Sutton Place.

Anyone with a sense of history cannot fail to have their imaginations fired by visiting any of these houses, where the great events of the past are brought alive in a still living fabric, not entombed in the dust of ages. Fate may occasionally seem to have intervened in the lives of their owners, but more often they made their own destiny.

I have tried in this book to chart their journeys through the centuries as the pendulum of Royal favour swung to and fro, and to show how their different paths crossed at many crucial junctions. They experienced, and did not always survive, unrest and revolt in the country, power struggles at Court, civil war at home, and foreign wars in Europe or across the seas. They brought home booty from abroad, and commissioned great works of art and architecture. This heritage is now shared with visitors throughout the summer months, and in the pages that follow I have tried to tell the interesting, and to me fascinating, stories that lie behind these imposing facades.

Exterior, the South Portico.

GOODWOOD

THE Goodwood estate, lying in the shadow of the South Downs just a few miles north of Chichester, has been in the possession of the Dukes of Richmond since 1695, when the First Duke bought what was then just a hunting lodge for the sum of £4,100. But the house that slides into view as you emerge from the tree-lined drive below it is largely the creation of the 3rd Duke in the last decade of the eighteenth century. His grandiose plans were originally for a huge octagon-shaped house, but he ran up so many debts that he only completed the three wings that we see today, much to the relief of his present heirs who believe that the maintenance costs of the other five wings would have been so prohibitive that by now Goodwood would have been a ruin.

The 9th Duke, now in his eighties, retired from the Chairmanship of the Goodwood Estate in favour of his son, the Earl of March, in 1969. An accountant by training, Lord March runs what is now not just an historic house but also a flourishing business concern. It is usually open to the public for only two days a week in the Summer because it is so in demand for business meetings, seminars and product launches, as well as all kinds of social occasions throughout the year. Some of these are in connection with the regular race-meetings at Goodwood Racecourse, the International and other Dressage Championship which are Lady March's special concern, or other cultural events such as the annual Chichester Festivities which began at Lord March's instigation. The family has played an influential part in the social, cultural and political life of Chichester and West Sussex since the eighteenth century, a tradition which the present occupants of Goodwood House still maintain.

It is significant that the 3rd Duke's magnificently imposing stable block, nearly as large as the house itself, was built before the house was enlarged. Designed in 1757 by Sir William Chambers, who also built Somerset House in London, it surrounds a quadrangle which is entered through a Tuscan arch more appropriate to a palace, and underlines the importance attached to horses at Goodwood from that day to this. Although Chambers was also commissioned to build the new house, the work later passed to James Wyatt. The 3rd Duke planted over a thousand cedars of Lebanon whose survivors still dominate the parklands of the estate, and he created on top of the

Left The 9th Duke of Richmond (right) and his son the Earl of March.

Below The Stable Block, designed by Sir William Chambers in 1757.

Downs the original racecourse which so many people think of first when they hear the name of Goodwood.

The Richmond family is descended in a direct line from Charles II through his liaison with Louise de Kerouaille, and their portraits hang side by side in the Ballroom. She was sent over to the English Court by Louis XIV to spy on Charles II, and as the present Lord March points out, 'she was pretty successful because she got so close to Charles II that she gave birth to a son by him; not bad I think in terms of achieving your objectives.'

Royal affairs were conducted so much in the public eye that Lord March even knows where his forebear was conceived – at a seat of the Duke of Grafton (another illegitimate offspring of Charles II) at a place called Euston Hall near Newmarket, 'but the significant factor for our family is that it was in an evening between two days racing at Newmarket, so horseracing was built into the family blood from the start.'

The portraits that gaze down at the visitor in the ballroom repay interest in what happened both to the subjects and to the pictures themselves. By far the most dominant is the family group of Charles I and his Queen, Henrietta Maria, with the infant Charles II and Princess Mary. Painted by Van Dyck, the sadness in the King's face foreshadows not only his fate but the chequered history of the painting. Sold by Cromwell to the Duke of Orleans, it passed to his descendants until one of them was guillotined during the French Revolution, after which Robespierre's men sold it to an English banker, who sold it to the 3rd Duke of Richmond. Thus it has been through the hands of two royal families, one English and one French, and two revolutionaries, one English and one French. To display it properly the 3rd Duke had the ballroom ceiling raised several feet so that the first floor now stands above the bottom of the windows, as at Uppark.

Next to it hangs a unique Van Dyck of Charles II as a young man, with eyes that already look very knowing. A few paces further on we see him as King, and by now the eyes express that disillusion with the ways of men he acquired during the hard and wearisome years of exile. The Crown Jewels he holds are not the same ones in his father's picture, which were melted down by Cromwell, 'the old vandal', as Lord March calls him. The sense of continuity is heightened by the Louis XIV clock on a shelf below the Merry Monarch, which has ticked away the hours since that time as it still does today.

Charles II generously endowed his numerous illegitimate children with titles and estates, but he was not so successful at bequeathing his own cool judgment and those political skills which saved his own throne on more than one occasion. Two of his offspring face each other across the ballroom, and both of them came to a bad end in one way or another. Lord March is grateful that Louise de Kerouaille's son bought the Goodwood Estate but 'as

Left Charles II as a young boy, by Van Dyck. (The painter often did other copies of his portraits, but this one is unique.) *Right* Frances Teresa Stewart by Sir Peter Lely. *La Belle Stewart* as Minerva, the model for Britannia on the coinage of the realm since Charles II's reign. (Another portrait of her in contemporary dress hangs at Broadlands.)

for the rest of his life the less said the better, it was spent very largely in drunkenness and debauchery'. At least he knew he could not succeed to the Throne, but the Duke of Monmouth, Charles's eldest illegitimate son, foolishly tried to oust his uncle, James II, on his father's death, 'and came eventually to a very sticky end; I believe they had to take the axe to his head six times and even then the knife was still necessary'.

The sight of these two perpetual reminders of rash and impulsive behaviour may have served as cautionary examples to succeeding Richmonds, since they have displayed both taste and acumen from the 2nd Duke onwards. He was christened Charles to mark his Royal descent, a name continued through each succeeding generation, and he seems to have inherited some of his grandfather's precociousness, certainly most things seem to have come to him early in life. Married at eighteen, briefly an M.P. at 21, he inherited the title at 22, but died at the early age of 49. His marriage was one of convenience, to Sarah, the thirteen year old daughter of the Earl of Cadogan, to settle a gambling debt. He had not met her before the ceremony and did not tarry to see her after it but was immediately rushed off on the Grand Tour for three years. She remained with her father at The Hague where he was Ambassador, but the happy ending to the story would be implausible if it were not true. On his return her husband went straight to the theatre, where he was captivated by a lovely woman. Upon enquiry he learnt she was 'the reigning toast of London, the beautiful Lady March'; and the marriage was consummated that night. In 28 years of married bliss she bore him twelve children.

A keen sportsman, pioneer of the game of cricket, the Master of the Charlton Hunt, the 2nd Duke also created a great menagerie and kept meticulous lists of its progress: 'five wolves, 2 tygerrs, 1 lyon, 2 lepers, 1 sired cat, a tyger cat, 2 foxes, a Jackall, 2 Greenland Dogs, 3 vulturs, 2 eagles, 1 kite, 2 owls, 3 bears, 1 large monkey, a Woman tygerr, 3 Racoons, 3 small monkeys, armadilla, 1 pecaverre and 7 caseawarris.' (His approach to spelling even by the more permissive standards of the eighteenth century always seems to have been very individual.) The tourist appeal of this early example of a 'safari park' was not always as welcome then, and his steward grumbled in 1730, 'We are very much troubled with Rude Company to see ye animals, Sunday last we had four or five hundred good and bad.'

The menagerie did not survive him, but there are more permanent reminders of the Second Duke at Goodwood. One of the earliest patrons of 'Canales', better-known to us as Canaletto, he commissioned from him the two great views of London that now hang in the main Entrance Hall. They were painted from the windows of Richmond House on the Thames (the London family seat which burnt down in 1791 uninsured eventually to be replaced by Old Scotland Yard).

Infant mortality being what it was then, upon his death in 1750 he was succeeded by his seventh child, the fifteen year old Charles, who over the next half-century transformed Goodwood into what we recognise today. He inherited 1,100 acres and debts of £17,000, and by the time of his death in 1806 he had increased the estate to 17,000 acres and amassed a fortune. He fought in the Seven Years' War against France, became a major-general by the age of 26 and Ambassador to France at 30. There he began acquiring the beautiful collection of Sèvres china which is displayed in the Yellow Drawing Room. It is flanked by two portraits of the Third Duke, one by Chevalier Mengs and one by Sir Joshua Reynolds, (who was paid £37.16s.0d for his work), the flesh-tints of which have gone rather white as so often in Reynolds' portraits. In spite of this, it is Lord March's favourite picture in the house, perhaps, as he admits, because he admires his ancestor so much. 'He was a very big man in every sense, a real visionary who did so many different things – he formed the Royal Horse Artillery at Goodwood, he formed the Royal Ordnance Survey which charted the first maps of this

Above The Yellow Drawing Room, the Sèvres collection flanked by two portraits of the 3rd Duke of Richmond.

Right Lord March pointing out the Gobelins *Don Quixote* tapestries, purchased by the 3rd Duke in Paris in 1765.

country, he built the Martello Towers to defend us from the French, which you can still see in the Channel to this day. He even advocated universal male suffrage in the House of Lords in 1783, now that is fifty years before the Great Reform Bill.' The 3rd Duke was a great patron of the arts as well. He commissioned works of art from an early age. When he was only 23 he opened his London house to 'any painters, carvers, sculptors, or other artists and youth over 12 years of age, to whom the study of statuary might be useful', a pioneering move which is seen now as paving the way for the Royal Academy; he was a Fellow of the Royal Society, and a founder of the Royal Society of Arts. He was a patron of Stubbs, and the three large pictures of Goodwood scenes he commissioned now hang in the Long Hall. (Recognised as some of his finest work they featured prominently in the 1984 Stubbs Exhibition at the Tate Gallery.) Their quality and the 3rd Duke's taste, is underlined by their proximity to the earlier horse paintings of Wootton, commissioned by his father, which look stiff by comparison with the flowing genius of Stubbs.

The 3rd Duke's collection was based on his own eye, not that of others, whether it was the brush of George Romney, the Louis XIV furniture, or the Gobelins tapestries illustrating scenes from *Don Quixote*. The house he built

to hold all this is his enduring monument, even though it crippled him financially; when he died he owed some £180,000 worth of debts. Unfortunately the impulsive generosity that won him friends in the world of the arts tended to make him enemies in affairs of State. Power was still very dependent on royal favour, and when he was only 25 Richmond made a fatal mistake. He resigned his appointment as Gentleman of the King's Bedchamber because his brother, Lord George Lennox, was not given the army promotion he felt was his due. His superiors in the Army and politics were not allowed to forget the King's displeasure, heightened when the Duke's nephew and heir challenged the King's brother, the Duke of York, to a duel on Wimbledon Common. (Lennox's shot went through the Duke's wig at twelve paces, and the Duke refused to fire, the insult being worse than the injury.)

Any chance of royal forgiveness was blown to the winds when Richmond committed his most spectacular act of defiance in 1783, by sailing his yacht flying the flag of the rebellious American colonists through the Royal Squadron drawn up for Review in Southampton Water, which took him perilously close to treason. More concerned with being right than politic, he aroused Edmund Burke's admiration, who said he was 'very full of rectitude, zealous against abuses, a little teizing in his disposition, and of little management with the world'. Another M.P., less charitably, exploded 'if there were two Dukes of Richmond in this country, I would not live in it'.

The Duke completed as much of the building of the house as he could afford in the last decade of the eighteenth century, and then decided to lay down the Racecourse, which held its first meeting in 1801. A strange event to today's racegoer, the horses ran several heats on the same day, so stamina was at a much greater premium than sprinting. From the beginning, racing at Goodwood has been very popular, and by the middle of the nineteenth century, after all the improvements made by the 5th Duke and his friend Lord George Bentinck, an eye-witness wrote 'a stranger would indeed be fastidious who did not consider Goodwood Course the perfection and paradise of racegrounds'.

In the Long Hall there is a large picture of the Lawn at Goodwood in 1886, showing 66 identifiable members of the cream of Society, from the Prince of Wales and members of his family, to other members of the aristocracy including the 7th Duke of Richmond, and stage celebrities such as Adelina Patti, Gilbert and Sullivan, Forbes Robertson, Squire Bancroft, and Madge Kendal. 'Glorious Goodwood' has remained a Royal favourite and has received many visits by the present Queen. A number of Privy Council meetings have been held in Goodwood House, including three by Queen Elizabeth II herself, because the July Meeting conveniently coincided with the end of the Parliamentary Session.

The Lawn at Goodwood, 1886. The Prince of Wales (foreground centre), and below his left elbow, Gilbert and Sullivan and Adelina Patti.

The 3rd Duke died a widower with no legitimate heirs, but one illegitimate daughter who was recognised and whose portrait hangs in the house, and after his wife's death three more daughters by the housekeeper. So the titles and estates passed to his nephew, aged 42, who had by now fought a second duel. Very much a soldier, the memories of his Dukedom at Goodwood are mostly of a military connection, particularly with the Napoleonic Wars, where he served as a special envoy in Brussels, while three of his seven sons served on the Duke of Wellington's staff.

One of the few short periods he actually spent at Goodwood was during Napoleon's incarceration on Elba. The Duke entertained the Russian Tsar and other European monarchs to a sumptuous breakfast in the Dining Room, but their celebration of Napoleon's defeat proved to be premature, and a much more famous occasion is now associated with the 4th Duke and his Duchess. At the behest of the Duke of Wellington, in order to deceive the enemy, they gave the famous Ball on the eve of the Battle of Quatre-Bras, three nights before Waterloo, and the picture recording a scene at the Ball is treasured by Lord March: 'The Duke and Duchess are receiving their guests in the background, the Duke of Wellington is being told by his Aide that Napoleon is on the move, next to the Duke of Brunswick who was slain by noon the following day on the field of Battle. Lounging in the chair on the left is the Prince of Orange, whose Aide was my ancestor, the Earl of March,

21

The Dining Room.

talking to a young girl. We don't know who she is, but she is about the same age as Lady Sophia Cecil, a young member of our family; and I remember my grandmother before she died telling me that she once talked to a very old lady, who was Lady Sophia Cecil, and she told my grandmother what happened at the Ball, and my grandmother told me.'

Fear of a French victory ran high in Brussels for the next three days, and perhaps out of relief as much as gratitude its citizens later presented the Duchess of Richmond with the Waterloo Service, a beautifully-painted set of porcelain showing various buildings in the vicinity of Waterloo, soldiers in the different regiments who fought in the battle, and one piece – a cup – which shows Goodwood House itself. It lacks the flagpole, chimneys, and magnolias that we see today, but in every other respect it is exactly the same. The Duke observed the terrible carnage at Waterloo as a civilian spectator, (rather like Tolstoy's Pierre at the Battle of Borodino). He died in agony after a bite from a rabid pet fox in Canada where he had been sent as Governor-General in 1818.

22

The Goodwood Cup in the Waterloo Service, presented to the Duchess of Richmond by the citizens of Brussels after Napoleon's defeat at Waterloo.

After his largely absentee Dukedom serving his country abroad the pendulum swung back with the 5th Duke (a swing we shall see repeated in many different ways as we retrace the family steps in the other houses in this book.) Although he too led an active political career on the national stage, he is best remembered for his great development of the Racecourse. In 1839 he celebrated his son's coming-of-age with a huge bonfire on the Trundle, the hill that looks down on the winning post, 'which from its elevation shed its brilliancy for miles around'. That scene is echoed today every July with the Fireworks Concert that is held on the Racecourse as part of the Chichester Festivities.

The meetings were originally held in March, but apart from the effect the unpredictable weather must have had on the spectators, Lady March believes that the date was probably changed to July because of the going. 'It would have been very heavy early in the year. We get a lot of low cloud and it really sits down on the hill and it gets very, very damp.' The change to July has been a lucky one – Glorious Goodwood almost always lives up to its name. Lady March can only remember one year when the meeting had to be cancelled because of wet weather. The new Grand Stand that was opened by the Queen in 1981 at a cost of over £4 million continued a long chapter of rebuilding and renovation on the estate that Lord and Lady March began in 1966.

The work in the house took three years and as it had not been lived in for twelve years everything needed doing. Lady March remembers that 56 rooms were done in the end, 'all the wiring and all the plumbing, and every wall and chair re-covered'. They knocked down all the old kitchens, sculleries, and rooms that needed endless scrubbing, with stone floors that were too bumpy for machines. But not all the decisions about restoration were so easy. One that remains unresolved is over the Louis Quinze chairs in the Tapestry Room. They still have their original covers which have grown rather tattered and faded over the last 250 years, and the family is currently

The New Stand at Goodwood Racecourse.

Above, page 13. Exterior, south side, showing the distinctive pepper-pot domes.

Right, page 17. The 3rd Duke of Richmond, painted by Sir Joshua Reynolds in 1959 for the sum of 30 guineas (with an additional 6 guineas for a miniature copy).

Top, page 17. The Thames from the Dining Room of Richmond House, by Canaletto. *Above*, page 19. The 3rd Duke of Richmond's Racehorses at Exercise, by George Stubbs. (The central figure with the Duchess is now thought not to be the 3rd Duke himself, but his bailiff and Steward, Richard Buckner.)

Above left, page 40. The Wedgwood Room.
Above right, page 43. The Dining Room, with Van Dyck's lifesize portrait of Charles I (top centre).
Right, page 43. The Drawing Room.

Top left, page 62. The Baron's Hall. *Top right*, page 52. The 17th Duke of Norfolk and his coat-of-arms, in the Drawing Room. *Above*, page 51. The Earl of Surrey defending his allegiance to Richard III after the Battle of Bosworth – painted by the American artist Mather Brown in 1797.

considering whether it would be right to replace the covers with a semblance of how they looked originally, knowing that it can never be a totally true reproduction. (An interesting comparison in this dilemma can be made at Broadlands.)

At first the sheer size of the house rather dismayed Lord and Lady March's young children: 'When we first got here they all said "Oh Mummy it's not going to feel like home and we don't know where you are", and one of the reasons we put in a lot of telephones was to make it fairly easy to get in touch with one person or the other.'

Their youngest daughter was only two when they moved into the house. She found the Ballroom particularly fascinating, as her mother remembers. 'There's an enormous mirror down the end of the room. She used to start the other end and run towards it. You couldn't get her out of there!' However she gave Lady March some anxious moments as well. 'I had one awful night when she climbed out of her cot just after we had gone upstairs and the house was in darkness.' The family did not know where to start looking in such a

The Ballroom – Charles II (right), next to Louise de Kerouaille, parents of the 1st Duke of Richmond.

large and unfamiliar place, but when they went downstairs and turned on all the lights, they discovered the little girl struggling up the huge main staircase with her crayons, explaining, 'I just wanted to do my drawing'!

The handful of domestic staff is less than a tenth of the number that used to be there so the lady of the house does her fair share of the work. She says it is a common sight to see her with a vacuum cleaner, especially after family weekends: 'I say I'm really the tweeny now who has to fill in when everybody else is off. One has to be able to do anything from cooking to shutting up the house or cleaning or whatever.'

A modern kitchen has been installed to cater for the large banquets and receptions, and the family entertaining, whether social or business, is determined by numbers: 'We have twelve in our dining room, upwards to about 28 in the State Dining Room, and after that we have to go to the Ballroom.' The State Dining Room is used about fifteen times a year on big occasions like the July Race Meeting and the International Dressage Championships, but Lord March says, 'I can't somehow see my wife and I sitting at either end of that table every night like my grandfather and grandmother did,' so they converted the Butler's sitting room for normal family meals.

The public rooms are cut off from the family apartments in one wing so the two sets of activities can go on simultaneously without either being aware of the other. 'We can't hear when there's anybody in the Ballroom and we can't hear cars arriving, so it's not difficult from that point of view,' says Lady March. 'Also we feel, the house was built to entertain people in, to be used, so we're very, very happy that people should enjoy it and use it for what it was built for.'

One of the most relaxing and attractive of the private rooms is the small library with its balcony to reach the books on the upper level. Many of the volumes are old and historic, and spring-cleaning there is a major operation: 'It means taking every book out and dusting it, and sometimes they have to be oiled, but the cleaning is a very big headache; we have to get everybody together at once, at least six people with special hoovers and machines that go up all round the tops, and we have a small scaffolding on wheels that's moved around.' At the same time it is a family room, 'usually full of school homework and bits of this and that' that Lady March's children have left behind them. And she admits that the balcony 'gets rather different use to what it was put there for', as the children love to run round and round it, and even their pet Siamese cats use it as a slide.

The Goodwood approach is very much of the twentieth century and Lord March is following the modern thinking of his father, the 9th Duke, a pioneer of the two technological advances that have transformed our way of life – the motor-car and the aeroplane. He learnt to fly in 1929 when navigation still consisted of following railway lines, and in 1936 opened a

The small Library.

small airfield at Goodwood which later became an RAF satellite station for Tangmere during the last war. He became a well-known racing driver in the late twenties and early thirties as Freddie March, with victories at Brooklands and other circuits, so it was perhaps only natural after the war that he should think of adapting the airfield perimeter at Goodwood for motor-racing. From 1948 to 1966 it attracted the great names of the sport, Fangio, Salvadori, Mike Hawthorn, Reg Parnell, and Stirling Moss who had a string of victories here until the spectacular crash which led him to give up competition.

But as the Duke of Richmond ruefully explained, unlike horses, cars were getting faster and faster every year. The boundary was too close to the track for safety when cars could reach speeds of 140 miles per hour on the straight, only a few feet off the main road. 'I'd been watching this for some time and I said, "I'm afraid there's only one way out of here, otherwise we are going to have a holocaust."' The track is only 2.4 miles round and he feared an

31

inevitable accident involving spectators like the Le Mans disaster that killed 80 people. So after eighteen years, the field has reverted to its former use and is the home of the Goodwood Flying School and Club, though the perimeter track is still sometimes used for test-runs and sprints and for films.

Adaptability and wish to move with the times are characteristics of the Richmond heirs. Over the last three centuries, they have made Goodwood a focus of political, military, social and sporting activity that has enriched the lives not only of the inhabitants of Sussex, or even of Britain, but of the rest of the world too. To visit Goodwood today is to realise the strength of Lord March's view 'that it's not a museum, that it didn't all happen in the past, that history happens here today'.

BROADLANDS

BROADLANDS, set by the river Test near Romsey in Hampshire, is perhaps best known to the public today as the home of the late Lord Mountbatten of Burma. It was here in 1947 that the Queen (then Princess Elizabeth) began her honeymoon with Prince Philip, as did the Prince and Princess of Wales in 1981. The house has been popular with royal visitors from the time of James I, but really came into its own when it became the home of the Viscounts Palmerston, especially the 3rd Viscount, whose presence can be felt in the house almost as tangibly as Lord Mountbatten's.

One man in his time . . .

Lord Mountbatten at Broadlands.

Today it is the home of Lord Romsey, Mountbatten's grandson, who inherited the house on his grandfather's tragic death in 1979. The royal connections are close still – Prince Charles was best man at Lord and Lady Romsey's wedding in 1979, the Princess of Wales is a godmother to the Romseys' daughter Alexandra, while Lord Romsey is Prince William's godfather. Lord Romsey is a film and television producer and his wife was an art restorer before her marriage. Since 1979 they have modernised and re-decorated the house and its furnishings, while at the same time trying to preserve the best of its unique character and historical associations. They open their home to the public for six months of the year.

Most of what the visitor sees today retains the unmistakable look of the eighteenth century. The original manor and the 'broad lands' surrounding it were owned by Romsey Abbey from before the Norman Conquest until Henry VIII's Dissolution of the Monasteries in the sixteenth century. Edward VI granted it to his uncle, Admiral Seymour, from whom it passed through the St Barbe family to Humphrey Sydenham. He never actually lived there and when he was ruined by the South Sea Bubble he sold Broadlands to Henry Temple, the 1st Viscount Palmerston in 1736. The first thing he did was 'to remove the farmer out of the house and his stinking yard after him'.

He then began the de-formalising of the gardens down to the river and soon found that 'this place altogether pleases me above any place I know'. But the great transformation was achieved by his grandson who succeeded him as the 2nd Viscount Palmerston at the age of eighteen. Fired with enthusiasm for the 'Grecian Taste and Roman Spirit' which the European Grand Tour often aroused in young men of his generation, he commissioned Lancelot 'Capability' Brown to re-design the house as well as the gardens. He must have been one of Brown's favourite clients – writing in 1767 that he had 'only settled the plans with Brown and have left everything in the execution of them to him', and the final account, totalling £21,150 in 1779, was submitted by Brown with 'thanks for numberless civilities, kind usage and pleasant imployment'. Much of the work on the house was completed by Brown's partner and son-in-law, Henry Holland, but his marvellous eye for the overall composition of a view led Brown to choose the white brick and Portland stone for the exteriors that make Broadlands blend so happily with the landscape. (According to Repton, Brown believed 'a red house puts the whole valley in a fever'.)

The visitor today enters the house through the four huge pillars of the East Front into the Domed Hall leading on to the Sculpture Hall, designed to hold the collection of Roman and Grecian sculptures gathered by the young Viscount during his Grand Tour. It is easy to understand his exclamation that 'what gave me the greatest pleasure was the ancient marbles. . . . I never saw a statue worth looking at until I crossed the Alps'. However, some he

The West Portico, overlooking the River Test.

brought back were contemporary eighteenth century pieces in the ancient style, and Lord Romsey's own favourite is the 'Boy on a Dolphin' copied by Joseph Nollekens from an original by Michelangelo now in the Hermitage in Leningrad. Lord Romsey explains that 'it tells the story of a young boy who befriended a dolphin. One day they were playing in the sea and the dolphin's fin gashed the boy in the side, you can actually see the wound and the blood coming out. The dolphin gathered up the boy and carried him desperately to the shore line; on arrival the boy was dead, and so the dolphin tossed himself on to the beach and died as well'. The sadness of the story somehow seems to enhance the beauty and delicacy of the sculpture.

The 2nd Viscount was never a rich man, his income varied between £7,000 and £12,000 a year during his lifetime, and although he was an M.P. for 40 years he only held minor office briefly, so his achievement at Broadlands is the result of careful planning and a connoisseur's eye. His more famous son, the 3rd Viscount (1784–1865), who became Foreign Secretary and Prime Minister, was fortunately far too busy with his public and private affairs to do very much to the house, since his only major addition was a large and rather ugly wing added to the Library. Lady Mountbatten had this demolished in 1954, as it was so out of character with the classical mid-Georgian look of the rest of the building.

Palmerston certainly had the most phenomenal energy. Apart from working long hours in office he was a well-known womaniser even in his eighties, often conducting several liaisons at the same time. He wrote in 1834, 'the life I lead is like that of a man who on getting out of bed every morning, should be caught by the end of one of the arms of a windmill and whirled round and round till he was again deposited at night to rest'.

In the Palmerston Room at Broadlands there are several evocative reminders of his stamina. It contains one of his high desks, where he worked standing up for hours on end, so that if he fell asleep from fatigue the fall would awaken him. Facing it is his portrait on horseback, outside the House of Commons, by Henri Barraud. Palmerston was a keen horseman who rode nearly every day, 'every other abstinence will not make up for abstinence from exercise' he insisted. When his business at Westminster was finished on Friday afternoons, he would mount his horse or use a light Carriage and head for Hampshire. The journey to Broadlands would take him between seven and eight hours.

Here too hangs the picture of the great love of his life, Emily Lamb. They were lovers for many years during which time she lived on the estate until her husband Lord Cowper died and they were at last able to marry in 1839. Since discretion had never been a particular virtue of either of them their marriage, although generally welcomed, caused not a little amusement. One friend wrote 'How strange will be Palmerston's Honey-Moon! There will be

Right Lord Palmerston's stand-up desk. *Left* Boy on a Dolphin, carved by Joseph Nollekens in 1765. *Bottom* Henry John Temple, 3rd Viscount Palmerston, by Henri Barraud. The Prime Minister is on horseback outside the Palace of Westminster.

nothing new about it except the marriage vow which they both know does not bind them'. Queen Victoria wrote happily to Prince Albert giving him the news, 'They are, both of them, above fifty, and I think that they are quite right so to act, because Palmerston, since the death of his sisters, is quite alone in the world and Lady C. is a very clever woman, and *much* attached to him; still I feel sure it will make you smile.'

Emily Lamb, by John Lucas, 1840. She was sister to one Prime Minister, Lord Melbourne, and wife to another, Lord Palmerston.

Emily and Palmerston enjoyed 25 years of married bliss with no recognised heirs. But Palmerston bequeathed Broadlands to the second child from her first marriage to William Cowper Temple; many people now believe, and Lord Romsey is certain, that Palmerston was the boy's real father. The estate then passed through his heirs to Edwina Ashley in 1939. She had married Lord Mountbatten in 1922; as a result much of great interest in the rest of the house is to do with their long occupancy and their busy public lives.

The North Staircase has been helpfully arranged to show the Mountbatten line of descent, which is intertwined with so many European royal families that Lord Romsey jokes, 'we're just a bunch of mongrels really!' They can trace the line back to Idolf in the fifth century A.D., but the first portrait in their possession, seen underneath the stairs, is of Phillip I, 'a Prince who organised the revolt in Germany in the sixteenth century with Martin Luther against Catholic domination, and the name Protestant comes from the fact that he drafted the legal protest against the alteration in the constitution which forbade them from practising their religion'.

On the first flight of stairs there are portraits of Louis VIII, the Landgrave of Hesse, and Louis IX. Lord Romsey draws attention to one special feature: 'You will notice that each has a peculiar lip; this was known as the Hessian lip and was a deformity I'm delighted to say has long since left the family'.

Other portraits on this staircase include two Crowned Heads in Lord Mountbatten's family tree – Queen Victoria, and Tsar Alexander II. But perhaps the most colourful and unusual illustrations of his Russian connection are to be found in the Coronation Books of the last three Russian Tsars. They are in the Oak Room, which leads off this staircase on the first floor. Several different periods nudge each other in this room, which still has its Jacobean interior of grained oak, with a large carved frieze in the style of Grinling Gibbons surrounding Lely's portrait of Lady Dorothy Sydney. The carvings are of the fruits of Broadlands – fish, fowl and fruit. The Oak Room, besides being one of the oldest rooms in the house, is also one of the most modern, for it can be transformed at the flick of a switch into a fully-equipped cinema, with a projection-booth and electrically operated curtains. When Lord and Lady Mountbatten went to Hollywood on their honeymoon they met many of the producers and stars, and Lord Mountbatten even made a short movie with Charlie Chaplin. From that time on he maintained a deep interest in the cinema, and a regular after-dinner entertainment for guests was a film show, a tradition kept up by his grandson today.

The royal and military connections of Lord Mountbatten are also very much in evidence in the Library, where he is pictured by Frank Salisbury on horseback in the Coronation Procession of King George VI. This is flanked by two portraits of him by Carlos Sancha, one in the uniform of Admiral of the Fleet beside the Portico at Broadlands, and one at Windsor Castle as Colonel of the Lifeguards. Lord Romsey remembers the room as being one of the most drab when he came to Broadlands. He had it redecorated and now it is one of his favourites. He uses it as his study and it is always a wrench when, at the beginning of the Open Season in March, he has to vacate it in order to allow the public to circulate easily through to the Wedgwood Room.

As its name implies the pale-blue shade of the walls in the room, with the friezes and mouldings picked out in white, are in the Wedgwood style, and it holds a collection of pottery begun by the 2nd Lord Palmerston. The most recent acquisition is a large portrait medallion of Lord Mountbatten struck in 1978, the year before he was assassinated. Lord Romsey points out that normally the subject gets a small copy, and there are only two large ones struck, one for the Pottery's records and one for presentation to the Queen. When the Mountbatten medallion was ready 'by chance the Queen was here, and the idea was that the Chairman of Wedgwood was going to give the large one to the Queen, and she was going to take it away with her. Somehow it stayed here, and another one had to be made at the factory and sent up to Buckingham Palace'.

During the last war Broadlands became an annexe to the Royal South Hants Hospital and the Wedgwood Room was used as one of the main wards. Patients could lie and gaze up at the beautiful moulded ceiling, and many of them have returned in recent years to see what was hidden from them under the 3-ply wood cladding which covered the entire wall area. Included in the boarding up were the bookcases, with all the books remaining in them.

The Oak Room, the only cinema with a Grinling Gibbons frieze. *Right* The Wedgwood Mountbatten medallion.

After the war, the room faced a less obvious but equally potent threat. Lord Romsey and his wife often have tea in this room, as he used to as a child. 'I remember particularly that both my brother and I were very messy eaters; my grandmother was extremely indulgent and allowed us to throw jam and goodness knows what else, over all the covers, much to the quiet horror of my mother.' One wonders what the reaction would have been of the splendidly imperious lady whose portrait by Lely hangs next to the window. She is Frances Teresa (La Belle) Stewart, and Charles II chose her to be the model for Britannia on his coinage.

The visitor with an interest in heads and silhouettes should be sure to visit the main guest-bedroom upstairs, known as the Portico Room since its windows are shaded from the setting sun by the overhanging West Portico. Moving to the windows to look out across the River Test valley it is worth examining the curtains rather more carefully than usual. It is then possible to see almost buried in the floral chintz pattern the thinly-traced profiles of the young Queen Victoria and Prince Albert, for the fabric was originally ordered for the Royal Yacht in 1854. These are matched by the silhouette profiles of the Queen and Prince Philip on the outside of the Kaiser porcelain Silver Jubilee vase displayed in this room.

View of the River Test from the Portico Room.

Next door is the Chinese Room, with the small desk where the Queen works at her papers when she visits Broadlands. The original hand-painted Chinese wallpaper of 1769 can still be seen behind hinged panels above the fireplaces, but now the room is lined with a brightly coloured modern floral pattern selected from Peking as recently as 1956 by King Gustaf of Sweden, Lord Mountbatten's brother-in-law. Here modern 'chinoiserie' has replaced the old, preserving at least the spirit of the original decoration.

One of the great dilemmas for the owners of the Grand Houses is what to do about soft furnishings which have deteriorated with age. Do you leave the original in a tattered state or should you throw away the original material and replace it with a modern fabric? The Romseys have managed some ingenious compromises. In the Wedgwood Room for example they cut and reduced the size of the curtains in order to re-use the fabric and so to 'beef up the remaining silk damask which you see on the sofas and the chairs; because the material is totally irreplaceable, there was no way we could get it woven again, and therefore we had no option'. Where that kind of ingenuity was impossible they simply decided to be bold and re-style rooms to harmonise with the existing features, with the help and advice of Lord Romsey's uncle, the interior designer David Hicks. The fruits of his work are particularly

The Wedgwood Room, with the Mountbatten medallion in the background.

striking in the Dining Room and the Drawing Room.

The Dining Room was originally designed by Henry Holland in 1788, and the sideboard and pier tables were designed to be positioned where they are today. Now, however, instead of Holland's original pastel colours of pale pink and green, they stand against a dramatic yellow on the walls, chosen by Lady Romsey and David Hicks. The Holland motif on the ceiling is echoed in a specially made Brussels weave carpet of bright blue and yellow.

The Dining Room at Broadlands is full of surface show concealing surprises. The ornate gold-painted grilles hiding the radiators are twentieth century, designed by Rex Whistler in 1935 for Brook House, the Mountbatten London home, and later installed here. Lord Mountbatten was always keen on the latest gadgetry and he had a Fabergé bellpush on the mantelpiece adapted to take a tiny ultra-frequency radio transmitter made by Ferranti to call the pantry. But Lord Romsey remembers that his ideas were not always such good ones: 'One of the more amusing sidelines for Lord Mountbatten was that shortly after the war, conscious of the fact that labour costs were ever rising, he was looking for various economies and he had the brilliant idea of going around all the beautiful seventeenth century clocks, taking out the old clockwork and inserting modern electric movements which needed no maintenance. When we inherited in 1979 we stumbled upon a crate full of ancient seventeenth century clockworks, which was fortunate because all the electric movements had long since seized up, and we have had a man for the last three years going round the house renewing, matching and balancing all the ancient clockworks.' There was just one clockwork left over with no case to put it in, so Lord Romsey got Garrards to design a case to go round it and gave it to his wife.

Lady Romsey again used the ceiling as her starting point for the redecoration of the Drawing Room. The circular centre-piece of the David Hicks carpet reflects Joseph Rose's intricate design for the ceiling, while the red and blue of Angelica Kauffmann's painted panels are echoed in the carpet and furnishings. This was one of the favourite rooms of Lord and Lady Mountbatten; here and in the Saloon next door there are many mementoes of them and the numerous famous visitors they entertained, including three who made a particularly strong impression on Lord Romsey as a small boy – Malcolm Sargent, Pandit Nehru and Noel Coward.

It was Noel Coward who drew attention to the difficulties of the plumbing in The Stately Homes of England. Broadlands' plumbing is agreed to be extraordinary by everyone. Lady Romsey still shudders at the problems she encountered whilst mastering the taps in her bathroom. There are no taps, in fact, and no plug either – only a series of what look like taps on the wall. You have to turn one to close the drain underneath and when the water level has reached about one inch it is difficult to tell whether the water is turned on or

Lord and Lady Romsey in the Drawing Room.

turned off. You have to watch it go and know which way the knob has been turned. She remembers running a bath once and being distracted and the next thing water was pouring down the dining room walls and all over the carpet. Fortunately no permanent damage was done.

Lord Romsey says that this used to happen continuously in Lord Mountbatten's day and caused no surprise. At one point his grandfather bought 'an expensive and hideous device which was attached to the bath and when the water reached a critical level it let out an almighty shriek that could be heard all over the house'. It was removed some years ago.

He tells what must be the ultimate in plumbing horror stories: 'My Aunt Pammy [the Mountbattens' younger daughter] had a mongoose as a pet, about the size of a squirrel, and at Broadlands we do have the most extraordinary plumbing with very large waste pipes. Well, this mongoose had rather a habit of getting into the plumbing, going down one plug-hole, and one particularly distinguished visitor was half-asleep in his bath one day with his feet up on the end, and up popped the mongoose out of the waste-pipe and bit him. He really did get a shock.'

Lord Romsey remembers with rather greater horror in hindsight a boy-hood accident to a priceless Sèvres rose bowl and ewer which had once

The Sèvres ewer and basin once owned by Marie Antoinette (and once broken by Lord Romsey as a small boy).

belonged to Marie Antoinette. 'At about five or six I was playing around in the corner of this room and I knocked this porcelain which shattered into a thousand pieces. There was a large party of grown-ups in the room and they all looked absolutely furious, but my grandmother didn't mind at all, she was totally non-material in every sense, she didn't care a hoot for material possessions.' Fortunately, someone cared enough for this one to have it painstakingly and invisibly repaired, and today the naked eye cannot perceive any cracks.

The three rooms on the West Front all look out over the River Test, which has always been famous for its fishing of salmon, trout, and the occasional pike. The fishing rights are now strictly controlled and licensed, but one of Lord Romsey's forebears disgraced himself there. 'Lord Mount Temple once saw a pike, got out the shotgun and actually shot a pike in the water, which is almost unheard of.'

The gentle slope down to the river sets off the imposing West Portico to full advantage with its four great pillars and pediment. Although it is in reality the back of the house it is the facade that everyone recognises, and it was on these steps that the Prince of Wales stood with his great-uncle, Lord Mountbatten, to open Broadlands to the public in 1979. Its aspect is impressive without being forbidding. In 1788 Lady Palmerston wrote in her diary, 'we came back and drank Tea by Moonlight in the portico and sat out till Ten'. Today Lord and Lady Romsey continue that tradition and eat out there in the summer as much as possible, 'and as the sun goes down all the bats which live above our heads there come out and catch flies and whisk around, which is lovely'.

There has never been a shortage of company at Broadlands: in the 2nd Lord Palmerston's day it was known as 'a kind of enchanted castle, where there were regular reunions of the first society'. Today many of the thousands of visitors who come here every year are drawn by the memory of Lord and Lady Mountbatten, and one of the main attractions is the Exhibition of their Life and Times in the old Stable Block. These memories of war and international upheavals only seem to enhance the contrasting peace and beauty of the place that has been home to two world-famous leaders, and the visitor soon comprehends what the magnetism was that drew them back here from the cares of office whenever their public duties permitted. But the appeal of Broadlands is perhaps best summed up by Emily Lamb soon after her marriage to Lord Palmerston: 'Nothing can be more comfortable than this House. It is magnificent when we have company, and when alone it seems to be only a cottage in a beautiful garden'.

ARUNDEL CASTLE

ARUNDEL Castle dominates the picturesque Sussex town that bears its name, a few miles east of Chichester. The Dukes of Norfolk acquired it in 1556 by the marriage of the 4th Duke to Mary Fitzalan, daughter and heiress of the 12th Earl of Arundel, and the Fitzalan-Howards have held it to this day, in spite of fluctuating fortunes. The present Duke is seventeenth of his line, succeeding to the title late in life in 1975 when his cousin Duke Bernard died leaving only daughters. Major-General Miles Fitzalan-Howard was a soldier for 30 years, starting as an anti-tank platoon commander in the Grenadier Guards in 1939. He had a distinguished war career from Dunkirk to the landings in Sicily and Italy, where he won the Military Cross, and the advance of the Guards Armoured Division from Normandy to the Rhine; after the war he commanded the King's African Rifles in Kenya, and the First Division of the British Army of the Rhine. The Duke remembers that his first visit to Arundel was actually during the war. 'It was straight after Dunkirk when I was Adjutant of the First Grenadiers, and 7th Guards Brigade came here about July 1940. The Brigade HQ was in the Castle, and my cousin Bernard asked the Commanding Officer, Colonel John Prescott, and the Adjutant, who was me, down to have supper with him in the Smoking Room.' Of course, neither of them had any idea that 'the Adjutant' would one day inherit the title. 'In no sense did I think it was going to work out like this.' In fact, they had to go right back to the 13th Duke to find a common ancestor, and as the present Duke explains, 'I'm actually more closely related to my cousin through his mother than through his father.'

Since his succession, the Duke has with his customary military briskness set about ensuring the future of Arundel for his son to inherit and for the nation to enjoy. The upkeep of the Castle had become a major burden and there was talk of presenting it to the National Trust, but instead the new Duke set up an independent charitable trust to manage the estate with himself as Chairman, and when he stays in his small apartment within the walls of Arundel he pays rent to the trust. He also has to spend time at his estates in Yorkshire, on his business interests in London, which include the presidency of the Building Societies Association, and on ceremonial affairs of State as Earl Marshal of England, 'the only one of the medieval Great Offices of State which still properly functions and has not been reduced to an empty honour'.

The family story must be one of the most dramatic in our history, enjoying Royal favour and high office at one moment, and suffering attainder, imprisonment and execution at the next. It is a theme that runs through both wings of the family, and the illustrations and mementoes of that history can still be seen at Arundel Castle today. The original estates in Norfolk which went with the title were long since sold or confiscated, and Arundel Castle has been the chief seat of the Dukedom for over four centuries. But there has been a castle on this site for much longer than that.

The oldest surviving part is the Keep, which dates from the Norman Conquest. In 1067, William rewarded Roger de Montgomery for looking

The Castle from the south.

after Normandy while William was conquering England, by creating him Earl of Arundel with estates covering a third of Sussex. The Keep surmounts a massive man-made mound, and as the Duke points out, with his General's eye, 'it's the most elementary bit of soldiering to see that if you hold this spur you obviously control the Arun Valley'.

But Roger's heirs did not hold it for long. His brother, Robert de Belesme, rebelled against Henry I, and the estates passed back to the Crown. In the twelfth century the Castle and lands were bestowed on the d'Aubigny family, with the title of Earl of Arundel and the office of Chief Butler of England which is still held by the Duke of Norfolk.

The Earldom of Arundel was later established 'in its original supremacy of honour above every other similar title of dignity', and its holders fought

The Keep, built between 1070 and 1090.

The Castle from the south west.

for the King in Wales, Scotland and France. One distinguished himself at Crecy, two died at Harfleur and Beauvais, others died on the block for rebelling against the King, but the Howard family they married into did all of that on a much more spectacular scale. In their rise to power the Howards made full use of all three major paths to noble status which the Middle Ages offered — the law, warfare and marriage.

The first Howard Duke of Norfolk was created by Richard III in 1483, with the additional titles of Marshal and Earl Marshal of England, Lord Admiral of England, Ireland and Aquitaine, and Deputy Governor of Calais. He has been accused sometimes of being involved in the murder of the Princes in the Tower, since one of them was the last Mowbray Duke of Norfolk, but this has never been proved. However, his fortunes were certainly bound up with those of King Richard, and the Duke rallied to his side when Henry Tudor landed in Wales to claim the throne.

Both King and Duke fell at Bosworth Field. The Duke's son was wounded in the battle, and was attainted by Henry VII, losing the Dukedom and most of his estates to the Crown. After three years of imprisonment in the Tower of London, however, he was released after swearing allegiance to the King.

That scene is graphically, if somewhat romantically depicted in a picture in the Barons Hall by the nineteenth century American artist, Mather Brown. He shows the young Earl of Surrey justifying his previous loyalty to Richard III in words which are a model of constitutional rectitude: 'Sir, he was my crowned King. Let the authority of Parliament place the Crown on that stake and I will fight for it. So would I have fought for you had the same authority placed the Crown on your head.'

The King needed him as the best military leader in the country, but he had to earn his way back into royal favour. Henry VII gradually restored the whole of his inheritance, reinstating the Earldom of Surrey, and finally the last of the family estates from his death-bed. To show how close they were Surrey was appointed one of the executors of the King's Will. He was by then Lord Treasurer of England, and with the accession of the new King he had to switch from the miserly caution of Henry VII to the flamboyant extravagance of Henry VIII.

Wolsey elbowed Surrey out of the King's special favour, so that he was left behind to guard the Kingdom when Henry and Wolsey journeyed to France. Soon after their departure James IV crossed the Scottish border with an army of 50,000 men and laid waste to Northumberland. Surrey raised an army only half the size but by brilliant tactics and superior artillery routed the enemy at Flodden, killing over 10,000 men including the Scottish King and the flower of the Scottish nobility, with the loss of only 400 men on the English side. For this great victory the 70 year old Surrey was at last 'honourably restored unto his right name of Duke of Norfolk'; and to mark

51

his outstanding military feat for the realm he was granted an honourable augmentation to his arms of 'a demi-lion rampant pierced through the mouth with an arrow', representing the lion of the Royal Scottish Arms chopped in half with an arrow stuck down its throat, a graphic if blood-thirsty memento of that victory, that can still be seen above the fireplace in the Drawing Room at Arundel Castle. (Very few noble families have such an augmentation – the Duke of Marlborough has one for Blenheim, and the Duke of Wellington for Waterloo.)

The 3rd Duke is the most famous, or infamous, of all the Howard Norfolks. He is said to be on anybody's short list for the 'Nastiest Man in English History' award, and even his descendants find it difficult to defend him. As the present Duke says, 'He is really most disreputable, a shrewd, cunning character, who was determined to maintain his family at the head of the kingdom, and he stopped at nothing to keep himself there. All his life he kept himself in power and one can't really be proud of the way he did it.'

His picture by Holbein in the long Picture Gallery at Arundel shows a severe face, his hair falling over his ears in a fashion long abandoned by his contemporaries, with a typical conservatism perhaps best exemplified in his outburst at a clerk in the Exchequer in 1540: 'I have never read the Scripture nor ever will read it. It was merry in England afore the new learning came in; yea, I would all thinges were as hath been in times past.'

For most of Henry VIII's reign Norfolk was the most powerful nobleman in the kingdom, but the power struggle at Court for the King's ear was unceasing, and failure could mean disgrace and often death. The Duke played the chief part in finally destroying both Wolsey and Thomas Cromwell, though not before the latter had put on the Statute Book his Treason Act of 1534, enabling a 'traitor' to be condemned to death without trial by Act of Attainder, an instrument that was to be used on a number of later occasions against the Howards.

To further his position Norfolk twice managed to provide Henry with a queen from his own family, but each time his triumph was short-lived and his subsequent conduct revealed the depths of his ruthlessness. His niece Anne Boleyn turned against her uncle after she became Queen, and when she was accused of adultery he helped prepare the charges against her, and then presided over her trial in his capacity as Lord High Steward. His other niece Katherine Howard only lasted a year as Queen before she too was accused of adultery, and Norfolk was one of the four Privy Councillors who cross-examined her. To save himself the Duke denounced her, shedding tears before the King to share his grief, and laughing when she was finally sentenced to die on the block, saying that he wished she had been burned at the stake.

His cruel streak was given free rein when he brutally suppressed the

THOMAS · DVKE · OFF · NORFOLK · MARSHALL
AND · TRESVRER · OFF · INGLONDE
THE · LXVI · YERE · OF · HIS · AGE

The 3rd Duke of Norfolk, 1473–1554, by Hans Holbein.

Catholic Pilgrimage of Grace. He persuaded the King to offer amnesty to the rebels and when they had laid down their arms he arrested the leaders of the rebellion and hanged nearly 250 of them. After one of his raids into Scotland to pacify the border it was said that he left 'neither house, fortress, village, tree, cattle, corn nor other succour of man'.

His enemies succeeded in trapping him at the end of Henry VIII's reign, and he was sentenced to death on a trumped-up Act of Attainder. But his luck of survival helped him right to the end. On the very morning he was due to be beheaded Henry VIII died, and his sentence was commuted so that the new reign should not open with the bloodshed of his execution. He remained a prisoner in the Tower for the whole of Edward VI's brief reign, but on Mary's accession in 1553 he was freed and restored to all his titles and estates, and died peacefully in his bed at the age of 80, once again the pre-eminent nobleman in the country.

The first three Dukes of Norfolk are the most famous because of their closeness to the Crown. Although none of them actually lived at Arundel their presence is very tangible in the long series of portraits lining the Picture Gallery upstairs, which runs the whole width of the Castle. Thomas Howard, 4th Duke of Norfolk and grandson of the 3rd Duke brought the Arundel estates into the family by his marriage in 1556 to Lady Mary Fitzalan, daughter and heiress to the 12th Earl of Arundel. Their pictures hang side by side in the Drawing Room. She died the following year at the age of seventeen giving birth to a son. Tragedy was to strike repeatedly at the Duke through his marriages, real and projected. His second marriage to another heiress, the daughter of Lord Audley of Walden, was a very happy one but only lasted five years before she also died, giving birth to his third son. His third marriage to the widow of the wealthy Lord Dacre was the shortest of all, when she too died in childbirth after only nine months, and this time the baby also died. Before that bereavement, however, the Duke had married off his three Dacre stepdaughters to his three sons, a remarkable marriage contract which secured for the Howard family the great northern estates of Castle Howard, Corby Castle and Greystoke.

But the marriage plan that brought about his downfall was the most overweeningly ambitious – to Mary Queen of Scots. She had fled to England in 1568, and Queen Elizabeth sent the Duke of Norfolk to York as one of the commissioners investigating whether Mary had been involved in the murder of her husband Darnley. The Duke became attracted to the idea of marrying Mary and restoring her to her Scottish throne. Unfortunately for him he lied about his intentions to Elizabeth in the most categorical terms:

> 'No reason could move him to like of her that hath been a competitor of the Crown; and if Her Majesty would move him thereto he will rather be

The 4th Duke of Norfolk, 1536–1572, after Hans Eworth.

committed to the Tower, for he meant never to marry such a person, where he could not be sure of his pillow.'

But the Tower was where he did end up, from a series of misjudgments of his Queen and her other ministers. He and Mary exchanged tokens, and a secret betrothal looked very close. Again he neglected to take the opportunity of telling Elizabeth and she began to suspect his loyalty to her. His enemies chose their moment, and used the Catholic scare of the Ridolfi Plot (a fabricated smear that was to be repeated in later reigns against later Howards), to trap the Duke in a trial with very suspect evidence. He walked to the scaffold on June 2, 1572. Ten years later his would-be fourth wife followed him to the block. The rosary Mary Queen of Scots wore to her execution is today one of the prized family inheritances to be seen at Arundel.

In a farewell letter from the Tower the Duke advised his son Philip: 'Beware of the court, except it be to do your prince service, and that, as near as you can in the lowest degree, for that place hath no certainty.' Prophetic words, for Philip Howard, Earl of Arundel, was also destined to end his days in the Tower, a Catholic at a time when allegiance to the Old Faith was considered akin to treason. He went to Court at the age of eighteen, ignoring his father's sound advice, and embarked on a busy round of dissipation, abandoning his wife to court the Queen's favour. But gradually he turned from his dissolute ways to a life of study, and particularly to a reconsideration of his religious beliefs.

The Long Gallery at Arundel Castle (now the Library) was the scene of his final conversion. He paced up and down its length and then, 'after a long and great conflict within himself', made up his mind to become a practising Catholic, for the moment prudently keeping secret the fact that he had been received back into the Church. But his changed demeanour from frivolity to seriousness provoked comment, and his reluctance to attend Anglican religious services at Court aroused suspicion, at a time when doubts about Catholic loyalty to a Protestant Queen were magnified into fear by the increasingly aggressive noises coming from Catholic Spain.

Philip Howard tried to flee the country by ship from Littlehampton, his own port at the mouth of the River Arun, but he was betrayed, arrested at sea and taken to the tower. The forged evidence was not sufficient to convict him for treason but he was fined £10,000 for attempting to leave the realm without the Queen's permission and imprisoned in 1585 during 'the Queen's Pleasure'. This proved to be a life-sentence, as further attempts were made to trap him into treasonable behaviour with other inmates.

In 1588 the Spanish Armada sailed against England, and the following year Philip was brought to trial again in Westminster Hall on a charge of

The Duke with the Rosary Mary Queen of
Scots wore to the scaffold.
The Library, formerly the Long Gallery.

having prayed for a Spanish victory. His sufferings in prison showed clearly in his face, but his wits were still keen enough to discredit the witnesses brought against him. Despite this a guilty verdict was brought in, but to such general revulsion that Elizabeth decided not to sign his death warrant, though the Earl was cruelly never told of his reprieve. So for the next six years he lived in suspense.

The harsh conditions of his confinement took their toll on his health, but seem to have deepened his faith. He spent hours on his knees praying, until his final illness, with its incurable dysentery which led to suspicions of poisoning, by which he was confined to bed and rapidly weakened. He petitioned the Queen for permission to see his wife and children, the younger of which he had never set eyes on; she agreed on condition he renounced his faith. He replied: 'On such condition I cannot accept Her Majesty's offers, and, if that be the cause in which I am to perish, sorry am I that I have but one life to lose.'

For his fortitude in adversity, and the unshakeable strength of his faith, he was canonised by Pope Paul VI in 1970 as St Philip Howard, one of the Forty English Martyrs. As head of England's foremost Roman Catholic family, the present Duke is particularly proud of his ancestor. St Philip's remains now rest in Arundel Cathedral, built in the last century at the time when so much of the Castle was restored, and these two great Gothic-style buildings dominate the skyline at Arundel.

St Philip's son, Thomas, is as highly regarded for his devotion to the arts as his father was for his devotion to religion. Known universally as 'the Collector Earl' he was the most important and influential of all the private patrons in the first two Stuart reigns, and is the present Duke's favourite ancestor. 'Perhaps one of his greatest claims to fame is that he and Charles I were really the beginnings of the European collectors of fine arts. He took Inigo Jones to Europe with him as his interpreter, Inigo Jones was very friendly with Palladio, and when Inigo Jones built the Queen's House at Greenwich that was the beginning of Palladian architecture, the end of Gothic architecture and really the beginning of the Renaissance in England.'

Partly his activities were intended to restore the glory and honour of the Howard family, which had been so reduced by the Royal prosecutions of his father and grandfather. The Dukedom remained under attainder during his lifetime but he was restored as Earl of Arundel and Surrey in 1604, and regained the Castle and some of the other confiscated estates. Two years later he married Aletheia Talbot who inherited from her father, the Earl of Shrewsbury, huge estates in the Midlands and the North, including much of what has since become the industrial City of Sheffield, the backbone of the family fortune ever since. His achievement in restoring the fortunes of the family is reflected in the successive portraits of him to be seen at Arundel –

Arundel Cathedral, built by the 15th Duke of Norfolk, completed in 1873.

the callow, rather awkward youth giving way to the imposing, bearded presence of his maturity. He began acquiring works of European art while on diplomatic missions for James I, and thereafter took every opportunity to travel abroad to enlarge his collection.

For the striking pair of paintings by Mytens he and his wife posed in the sculpture and Holbein galleries at Arundel House in the Strand, London, and these pictures now hang in the Drawing Room at Arundel Castle, facing the 4th Duke and his wife. But the Earl was instrumental in bringing an even greater Flemish artist to England, Van Dyck. A number of his paintings can still be seen at Arundel, including the 'Madagascar portrait' in the Barons Hall, a double portrait of the Earl and his wife, so-called because among the objects from the collection that surround them is a globe of the world on which the Earl is pointing at Madagascar. He was reputed to be considering emigrating there at the time, 1639, to escape his creditors, 'but he didn't in the end because he had an amusing report saying it was too full of fleas'.

By the following year his debts exceeded £100,000, a huge sum for those days, spent largely in accumulating his great collection of marble sculptures from the ancient world, antique gems, drawings, prints, woodcuts, engravings, and paintings by Raphael, Leonardo da Vinci, Holbein, Durer and

The 'Madagascar portrait' of the Collector Earl and his wife Aletheia Talbot by Van Dyck, 1639.

Parmigianino, and many books, including the great Pirkheimer Library bought from Nuremberg in 1636. Many of these have since been sold, or in some cases given away, like the last-named which the 6th Duke gave to the Royal Society, and the heraldic manuscripts which went to the College of Arms.

The library at Arundel Castle holds what is left of the books in the Collector Earl's once-enormous acquisitions, along with the 9th Duke's collection, moved here after the fire at his property in Worksop. One of the books which the present Duke finds of great interest contains details of all the Knights of the Garter. 'My ancestor, Sir Miles Stapleton, in my mother's family, was one of the founder knights, who was a friend of the Black Prince and used to joust with him. And it's rather amusing to think I've still got the same name as it's been handed down through my mother's family.' His mother showed a fondness for names beginning with 'M'. Having started with Miles, she continued with Michael, Marigold, Martin, Miriam, Miranda, Mirabelle and Mark.

The library is presided over by a Dieussart bust of Charles I, one of the few remaining items of the Collector Earl's art treasures. Charles looks as melancholy in marble as he does in many of Van Dyck's portraits, and the Civil War that ended his reign broke with particular force over Arundel. Parliamentary troops besieged it reducing much of it to ruins, and desecrated the Fitzalan Chapel by stabling their horses in it.

Restoration of the Chapel began in the nineteenth century, including the East Window whose stained glass now carries a picture of the 4th Earl of Arundel who built it, holding a model of the original chapel. One most unusual feature of the building is that the Fitzalan Chapel is a private Catholic place of worship only accessible from the Castle grounds, and beyond the screen to the West is the Anglican Parish Church. Although the two denominations are normally physically separated within one building the Duke took pains to celebrate the quincentenary of the Dukedom in 1983 with a properly ecumenical service in the Chapel, conducted by the Anglican Bishop of Chichester and the Catholic Bishops of Arundel and Brighton, processing from one half of the Church to the other.

As with many of the other great houses in this book, the process of restoration is unceasing, and the present Duke has put substantial repair works in hand since 1975. Two fifteenth century effigies in the Chapel, of William, 9th Earl of Arundel and his wife Joan Nevill, were recently brought down from the top of a tall, catafalque-like tomb chest where they had been invisible. They were cleaned by John Green and Michael Bailey, revealing the original late medieval decoration. 'The incredible colours come to life which haven't been made up by any falsification, and we're very very proud of this because it's almost unique to have so much medieval colour still left.'

Leaving the Chapel and crossing the drawbridge over the dry moat into the Castle the visitor enters from the inner quadrangle the low-vaulted Stone Hall, and ascends the stone staircase to the suddenly breathtaking vastness of the Barons Hall, fifty foot high and nearly three times as long. Built on the site of the original medieval hall in the nineteenth century it holds furniture of several periods, but most interesting are the reminders of the various political and religious intrigues and upheavals in which the Howards figured importantly.

The Baron's Hall.

Although the Restoration of Charles II was followed by the restoration of the Dukedom of Norfolk, which had been under attainder for nearly a century, royal favour was no longer sufficient protection. The first picture you see on entering the Barons Hall is of Cardinal Philip Howard. As a Catholic friar in Brussels he befriended Charles II in exile, was sent to England to negotiate the Restoration in 1658 and when his mission was betrayed just managed to escape in disguise. He returned with the King in 1660, negotiated his marriage to Catherine of Braganza at which he was the only English witness, and became her chaplain and Grand Almoner. As Almoner he was the only man in England allowed to appear in public dressed as a Catholic priest, but as the tide of anti-Catholic feeling rose in the 1670s he became the target of that hostility and was forced to leave the country for Rome in 1674. A year later Pope Clement X made him a Cardinal for his zeal on behalf of the Church in England.

Just before he left England Philip was instrumental in arranging another royal marriage, of Mary of Modena to Charles's brother, later James II. Both their pictures look down from the walls of the Barons Hall and, just as you can see the intelligence in Charles II's face at Goodwood, you can see the lack of it in James's at Arundel. As the present Duke says, 'Well, James II was an impossible man wasn't he? His intolerance led him into the hopeless position of the Glorious Revolution of 1688.'

But the Barons Hall is above all a monument to the initiative and energy of the 11th Duke who succeeded to the title in 1786. More popularly remembered as the 'Drunken Duke', the full-length Gainsborough portrait in the Drawing Room bears out the contemporary description: 'Nature which cast him in her coarsest mould, had not bestowed on him any of the external insignia of high descent. His person large, muscular, and clumsy, was destitute of grace or dignity.'

His nickname was an accurate one. His annual drinking-bouts with the Prince Regent so alarmed Mrs Fitzherbert that she tried her best to stop them, with only limited success. There was one famous occasion when for a joke the Prince got the 11th Duke into such an inebriated state that 'he put him back in his coach and the coach drove round Brighton so that when he woke up he was still at Brighton and had not come back to Arundel at all!' Averse to soap and water, the Duke could only be bathed by his servants when he was insensible from drink. His wife went insane soon after their marriage but outlived him so he left no heirs. But a succession of mistresses produced many offspring. The present Duke remembers a family story of his ancestor arriving by coach at Greystoke Castle; it was surrounded by children so the Duke asked his coachman, 'Who are all these children?' The coachman replied, 'Some are mine Your Grace, and some are yours Your Grace.'

Cardinal Philip Howard, 1629–1694 by Blanchet.

But for all his weaknesses of the flesh he is remembered gratefully at Arundel for his rebuilding of the Castle, which occupied the last 25 years of his life. He chose as his architectural style a hybrid of perpendicular Gothic and Norman which was associated in his eyes with ancient liberty, and dedicated the foundation stone of the Barons Hall in 1806 to 'Liberty asserted by the Barons in the reign of John', hence its name. It housed a lavish banquet to celebrate the 600th anniversary of Magna Carta in 1815.

He laid out the park which now surrounds the Castle and opened it to the public as soon as it was finished. They could also visit the Castle itself one day a week for a small charge, which was then given to the poor. His rebuilding achievement alone is enough to make him a memorable Duke of Norfolk, but that was only a part of his life. He was a great radical, a friend of Fox, an opponent of the slave-trade, and a supporter of the Parliamentary motion 'that the influence of the Crown has increased, is increasing and ought to be diminished'. But he defended his membership of an unrepresentative Chamber in a characteristic manner: 'I cannot be a good Catholic; I cannot go to Heaven; and if a man is to go to the Devil, he may as well go thither from the House of Lords as from any other place on Earth.'

It is therefore not perhaps surprising that as you leave the Barons Hall and traverse the Picture Gallery you come to what was once the Chapel, but which the Drunken Duke converted into the Dining Room. The fan-vaulted ceiling gives the room such a chapel-like atmosphere that to try and dissipate this the Duke put in a huge stained-glass window showing an amply-endowed Queen of Sheba being entertained by himself as King Solomon. Unfortunately this was taken out again before Queen Victoria's visit in 1846 in case she was 'not amused'. The dining table is set with the family porcelain and silver-gilt wine-stands supported by the Fitzalan horse and the Howard lion. As the present Duke explains, 'We never have our meals here at all; we have them in a little flat upstairs', but it is occasionally used, as when the Duke entertained President Arap Moi of Kenya here during his state visit to this country. But this room does prompt him to point out that the Drunken Duke had one lasting impact on our eating habits because of his great love of entertaining at length. 'He's famous for having changed the major meal of the day from three o'clock, which is what happened in the eighteenth century, to half past six in the evening.'

Despite his lapses he is more responsible for what survives at Arundel than many of his more illustrious forebears. His opinions may have wavered throughout his life, it was whispered at the end that 'he refused seeing a priest of the Church of Rome in his last moments, although it had been repeatedly proposed to him', but his legacy at Arundel is monumental.

Later Dukes have been rather stronger Catholics, and the fifteenth of his line built the Catholic Cathedral at Arundel in memory of his father whose faith so dominated his life that he devoted it to good works for his less fortunate co-religionists. The 15th Duke was in many ways the reverse side of the coin from his ancestor the 11th. Bereaved young he drowned his sorrows not in drink but in architecture. He restored the oldest parts of Arundel Castle with great attention to historical accuracy, and where the Drunken Duke's work had left a sometimes unfortunate mixture of eighteenth and nineteenth century Gothic he swept it away to recreate a more coherent re-creation of how a medieval castle should look.

But interesting as the architecture is, and beautiful though the pictures are, the great fascination of Arundel is the brooding sense of history, and the significant part the Howards have played in it. In one of his battles with the Committee of Privileges the Drunken Duke was once criticised for being 'too much engrossed by the phantom of the exclusive greatness of the Howards'. His descendant the 17th Duke is just as conscious of the dark side of his inheritance. One of the antiquarian books in the library has a panoramic view of London, and he is fond of singling out one particular place in it: 'You can see the Tower where we've had rather a sad time, and it rather makes us shudder the same way that I think some people shudder when they hear Wormwood Scrubs, but we always shudder when the Tower is said because so many of our family have ended their lives there.'

The premier peer, Earl Marshal of England, possessor of twelve ancient titles including the only surviving dukedom of medieval creation, the present Duke is well able to put his unexpected inheritance into perspective. 'One's very proud to have had these things come to one, but I'm much more satisfied to have served in the Army for 30 years and to achieve things there than all these inheritances which I respect very much, but I think one's really got to be one's own self and try to do some good in the world.'

BREAMORE

BREAMORE House, three miles from Fordingbridge in Hampshire, was built in the shape of an 'E', like so many of the great Elizabethan houses, as a form of courtesy to the reigning monarch, and from the outside it still looks much as it did when it was completed four centuries ago. The view from the house is also little changed, east down the avenue of limes, south across the park to the ancient yews and cedars encircling the Saxon church, and south-west across the valley of the River Avon to the New Forest.

Much of the income of the estate today is still derived from farming, supplemented by a flourishing Countryside Museum, Crafts Fair, and Carriage Museum, as well as admission charges to the house and grounds. Although it is not as well-known as many of the other houses in this book, it has had its fair share of 'blood and thunder'. The present owner is Sir Westrow Hulse, but he has handed over the management of most of the affairs of the estate to his son, Edward, who combines this with his stockbroking business in London. The Hulse family has lived here since 1748, but they are very conscious of the chequered and often violent history of the house before it passed into their ownership.

There have been settlements here since pre-Christian times; on the Downs, beyond the wood that shelters the house to the north, can be seen a long barrow called the Giant's Grave and other ancient tumuli. But the first recorded entry is in the Domesday Book, where the manor of 'Brumore' is registered as a Crown demesne, part of the Royal manor of Rockbourne. The Saxon church already existed and the evidence proving its date was found in 1897, when an Anglo-Saxon inscription over the arch opening into the South transept was uncovered. It reads 'Her Sputeland seo Gecpyoraednec De' ('Here is made plain the Covenant to thee'), but its importance lies in the particular formation of the letter 'S', as Edward Hulse explains: 'On the left you see the pre-980 "S" which is like a "Z" reversed ("Ƨ"), and then further on you see the modern "S", so therefore we know that it must have been carved around 980, which is the date when the "S" changed in the English language.'

The manor passed through several hands, reverting back to the Crown on more than one occasion, and a priory stood on the site until the Dissolution

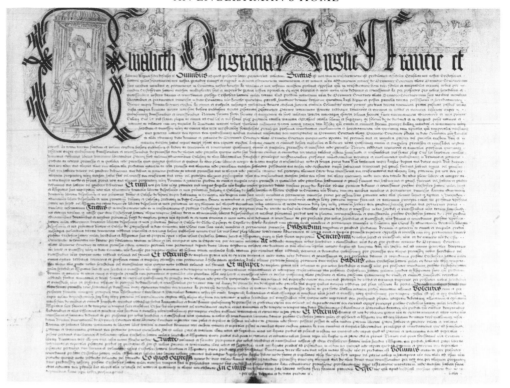

The original deeds of the House, rediscovered in 1982.

of the Monasteries. It was included in the dowry of two of Henry VIII's wives, Katherine Howard and Katherine Parr, passing to the latter's second husband, Thomas Seymour. When his brief glory as Protector of the young Edward VI was ended by his supplanting and execution it again reverted to the Crown. In 1579 Queen Elizabeth granted it to her Lord Chancellor, Sir Christopher Hatton (the original deed was rediscovered in 1982 and can now be seen in the Great Hall), but since his main residence, Holdenby House, was nearly as big as Hampton Court he sold Breamore within a year to William Dodington.

It was Dodington who built the house in 1583 that we see today, and considering what subsequently happened to him and his heirs it is surprising it is not haunted. His origins were obscure but his end was spectacular. Although his wife, Christian, was sister to Sir Francis Walsingham, Secretary of State and the Queen's spymaster-in-chief, Dodington was threatened with an action in the Star Chamber which so preyed on his mind that he committed a very public suicide by throwing himself off St Sepulchre's steeple in broad daylight. As Edward Hulse says, 'It caused quite a sensation in 1600!'

This suicide in the heart of Holborn was the first Act in a tragedy of three decades that might have been written by one of the Jacobean playwrights.

The William who succeeded his father was knighted at the time of James I's Coronation and in 1606 was made Sheriff of Hampshire. But in 1629 the family was the subject of shocked discussion among the high-born. Sir Henry Bourchier described in a letter to Archbishop Ussher how Henry Dodington, 'being reprehended for some disorderly courses by his mother, drew his sword and ran her twice through, and afterwards, she being dead, gave her many wounds; and had slain his sister at the same time, had he not been prevented'.

By this act Sir William lost both wife and son, for Henry was given the customary sentence, and local legend has it that 'the son for this horrible matricide was hanged in sight of the house where he was untimely born', although it seems more likely he was executed in Winchester Jail. From that date it is as if there were a family curse that cut off the male heirs before their prime. Four years later Sir William lost his eldest son, Herbert, his son John who succeeded him did not long survive his father, and John's daughter and heir Anne had several sons from her marriage to Lord Brooke, all of whom died young.

It is therefore perhaps not surprising that the only surviving family portrait is of the wife of the first William Dodington, in her widow's weeds looking very forbidding above a doorway. It was sold with the house to Sir Edward Hulse in 1748, whose namesake gives it rather a wide berth: 'There's a rather spooky story that if you touch the picture you die the same day. Two people have tried since the war; one did die the same day and the other didn't. So it's about even money, but I have never touched it, I don't like the odds.'

The superstition is clearly still a very powerful one. When the house was taken over by the American Army during the Second World War to become General Patton's Headquarters before D-Day, all its possessions were evacuated – with the exception of Christian Dodington's brooding presence, which nobody would move.

It is rather a relief to turn from the gloomy saga of the Dodington family to the much happier and fulfilled story of the Hulses. Their fortunes were founded on the medical skills of a notable father and son. Edward Hulse the elder lived from 1631–1711, 'a person of great skill in the practice of physick' who became Court Physician to William of Orange, and accompanied him to England when he became King in 1688. His son Edward inherited his father's Court position as Physician to three monarchs, Queen Anne, George I, and George II, who in 1739 made him a baronet. Portraits of the two doctors hang side by side in the Blue Drawing Room, bearing the confident mien of men sure of their position in uncertain times. As their descendant reminds us, 'their lives seemed rather safer because of course they had the knife'.

71

Christian Dodington – the painting no-one dares to touch.

The 1st Dr Hulse, 1631–1711, by John Riley.

The 2nd Dr and the 1st Baronet, 1682–1759, by Francis Cotes.

They also began the family tradition of marrying heiresses, a tradition which Edward Hulse freely acknowledges to have continued to this day, bearing in mind his own definition of an heiress as 'someone who carries achievements in her own right'. Back in the late seventeenth century, the elder Hulse married Dorothy Westrow, who acquired through her family many of the most interesting objects in the house, and the first baronet married Elizabeth, daughter of Sir Richard Levett, a Lord Mayor of London and Governor of the Bank of England. It is rather ironic therefore that in his old age Sir Edward developed a curious obsession that he would die in penury, and to try and assuage this fear the people who looked after him made a habit of slipping guineas into the pocket where he formerly put his patients' fees. He never actually lived at Breamore, which he bought for his eldest son, Edward, preferring to live out his retirement at the house in Kent which he had inherited from his father and bequeathed to Richard, his second son.

The second Sir Edward chose not to follow in his father's and grand-father's medical footsteps, but did follow their example in his marriage to Hannah Vanderplank, daughter of a City Merchant of Dutch origin. Por-traits of Hannah, her husband, and her father all hang in the Blue Drawing Room facing the two doctors, revealing that she was a great beauty as well as a great heiress. Her husband was known as the Handsome Sir Edward, by implied contrast with his father, and one can see why by comparing the two portraits. This room also holds the rather intricate Dutch marquetry furni-ture which was a wedding present to Hannah from her father, and two glittering examples of her own and her husband's taste – the Chinese Chippendale mirror over the fireplace and the Regency chandelier. The pair to the chandelier and a similar Chippendale mirror hang in the West Draw-ing Room, which the family now use as their private drawing-room when the house is closed to the public.

The third baronet's wife, Mary Lethieullier, brought him her father's estates in Essex and the collections of her uncle, the connoisseur Smart Lethieullier, though sadly much of the latter perished in the big fire which swept through the house in 1856. But her husband was very much over-shadowed by his younger brother Samuel. A picture by Thomas Hudson of both of them as small boys in fancy dress can be seen in the West Drawing Room, hand in hand. Samuel went into the Army, served under the Duke of York in Flanders, and became A.D.C. to the Prince Regent who 'went about with his three Colonels, Lake, Hulse and St Leger, in an endless whirl of gaiety and expense', in Sir Arthur Bryant's vivid phrase. The Prince marked his friendship by presenting a flattering portrait of himself to Samuel, painted by Thomas Beach, with the frame bearing the Prince of Wales's feathers.

Hannah Vanderplank, wife to the 2nd Baronet, 1735–1803, by Francis Cotes.

When he became King George IV, Samuel was appointed Treasurer of the Household, and knighted a year later. When William IV was crowned in 1830 he was made a Field-Marshal, and his red baton can be seen at Breamore, bearing the gold Lion and the gold St George and the Dragon. It is kept in the inner hall, just off the entrance hall, together with other military mementoes of Sir Samuel's time. There is a set of Napoleonic battle scenes by the French artist Beaufort, painted from sketches he made on the spot during the actual battles, so they have considerable historical interest as well as being attractive to look at. To redress the balance of all these French victories there hangs next to them a striking sketch in oils of the head of the Duke of Wellington. It was the Duke's favourite picture of himself because it shows him in three-quarter profile which diminished the sharpness of his famous hook-nose (which can be seen in its full impact at Stratfield Saye). The painter, Lucas, used this sketch as a study for the life-size equestrian portrait of the Duke at Herrenhausen, which he painted for the King of Hanover.

The Hanoverian connections of the Hulses are underlined by the large portrait of George I in his state robes, given to the first Sir Edward as a tribute to his medical skills and service to the two monarchs. This is more important to the family because of its royal subject and origins than because of its artistic quality, but other family acquisitions in the house are uniquely interesting in both subject and treatment.

Climbing the staircase to the Alcove on the first floor the visitor finds an extraordinary set of the first ethnological paintings ever produced, showing the products of marriage between Europeans and various Indian races in the New World. They were painted in Mexico by an illegitimate son of Murillo, and the children are shown as mulattoes, mestizas, and in one instance the union of a Moor and a Spaniard has produced an albino. The story of their journey to Breamore is just as exotic.

The brother-in-law of the first Dr Hulse, Norton Westrow, was one of Charles II's licensed privateers and was given, or assumed, the courtesy rank of 'Admiral'. Today Edward Hulse recognises that his reputation is open to dispute: 'In Seville there is a Spanish account where his title in fact is that of pirate and not Admiral, I rather naturally prefer to use the rank of Admiral.' Whatever the rank, the story is not in doubt. The Spanish galleon carrying the paintings as a gift to Philip II was seized on the high seas by Admiral Westrow for Charles II. 'Fortunately they were considered shocking because they show the mixing of blood, which was against all contemporary thought, and so the King luckily refused to have them, otherwise of course we'd never have got them at Breamore.'

Part of the same booty that Westrow gave to his niece Dorothy was an octagonal alabaster table-top, inlaid with silver and bearing an inscription in Spanish saying 'I serve my lord and master Don John Newton in Los

Napoleonic Battle scenes by Beaufort, based on his eye-witness sketches. *Top* Unfinished sketch of the Duke of Wellington, by J. Lucas.

Angeles', thought to be Puebla de los Angeles in Mexico. Whatever the Spanish intended the table for, Edward believes the English found another use for the alabaster pot that stands on it: 'The story goes that people used to put their stake on the little trays and rather like in poker if they lost or didn't want to go on betting they tipped their money into the pot, and the winner took the pot with all the money in it which belonged to him, and that's how the term "taking the pot" started.'

Another intriguing and unusual table, this time from India, has a reputed 128 different types of wood inlaid into its surface in a swirling circular pattern. It probably had a religious significance because it is decorated with the sign of Krishna around the outside edge.

The Admiral clearly had a keen eye for the rare and unusual, and he brought back from one of his expeditions a Mexican feather fan. Made from the feathers of Birds of Paradise and other birds, and richly decorated on both sides, it shows St George slaying the Dragon and other allegorical scenes. Unlike the handful of other such fans that have survived, it has retained its vivid colours to this day. 'Luckily the Hulses didn't realise how important an object it was and kept it in a drawer,' says Edward. 'So it was actually kept exactly as it should be, in the dark, and this is why we now exhibit it in a frame with doors that shut, so a good deal of the time it remains in the dark. When we discovered it the curator of the Museum in Munich flew to London and hired a taxi and came straight here before we could commit any sins.'

Another foreign acquisition in the Great Hall is a set of Chinese porcelain decorated with the Gosling coat of arms associated with the family, and the Chinese craftsmen who produced it were illiterate so the armorial paintings are not accompanied by the usual motto. Edward is particularly attached to a shaving bowl with an indentation to go round the neck, 'because it was said that Chinese girls could shave a man so well that they didn't even wake him when they did it. While one girl shaved the man the other girl put the bowl underneath his chin so a drop of water shouldn't fall on him and wake him up. I've always wanted to try it but I can't find the two Chinese girls I need to do it!'

The Great Hall is perfectly symmetrical: it is in fact four cubes, 21 feet high, 21 feet across and 84 feet long. It contains some unusually interesting pictures. One is of Sir Thomas Coningsby, an Elizabethan soldier, with his dwarf 'Crickit', and Gheeradts has disguised Sir Thomas's own deformity by painting him with his left foot resting on his pet dog, so that the casual observer does not notice that one leg is shorter than the other.

At the opposite end of the Great Hall is a rare full-length portrait by Cornelius Jannsens of Sir Norton Knatchbull, namesake and ancestor of the present Lord Romsey, as well as of the Hulses. The landscape glimpsed

The Chinese porcelain in the Great Hall
Left The Shaving Bowl, 'for use by two
Chinese girls'.

through the window behind Sir Norton gives a typically Dutch flavour to the portrait, reminding us of the importance of that country to the family's fortunes. Next to it is another ancestor, Lord Coventry, wearing his robes of office as Keeper of the Great Seal to Charles I and prudently keeping his hand on the Privy Purse.

On the long wall facing the windows is 'The Coming of the Storm', by David Teniers the Younger. It shows villagers feasting outside an inn with a storm brewing in the distance, and is a narrative picture full of detail. One of the best pictures in the house, it is also Edward Hulse's favourite: 'It's a kind of caricature, each person is really a portrait in its own right and I love looking at them. The man dancing with the girl in the centre, who is in fact Mrs Teniers, the rather bored man who's obviously come out to fetch wine, the slightly lecherous man, another one with his hand round the girl's waist, you can even see a man being sick at the back.'

Edward Hulse, beside *The Coming of the Storm*.

The sight of so many people feasting leads the visitor almost automatically to the Dining Room that opens off one end of the Great Hall. It still has the original Elizabethan fireplace with the stone strapwork of that period and the Tudor Rose and Crown in the middle, but the heavy oak table is older, dating from the fifteenth century. Edward likes to think that it came from the Monastery that stood here until the Dissolution: 'You can see the monk's heads carved at the foot of the table, and indeed the places where the monks ate, as they didn't have plates in the fifteenth century, and ate straight off the table.'

The original Elizabethan fireplace in the Dining Room, with its distinctive strapwork.

His family still eat here (using plates of course), in the winter when the house is closed to the public, surrounded by four large canvases of dead game in landscapes painted by Peter Andreas Rysbrach. Much admired in the painter's lifetime they must have faded in their appeal later, since Sir Edward Hulse bought the set for only £5 in 1765, but they are now of considerable value and local interest, as they show the Great English Bustard which became extinct in the eighteenth century. These birds used to be fairly common around Breamore, and now Aylmer Tryon and the Great Bustard Trust are trying to breed them again not far away.

The Dining Room.

83

As so often in these large houses the Kitchen is a long way from the Dining Room. When Sir Westrow was living here his wife used a pedometer, and was not surprised to discover she was walking three miles a day within the house. Neither she nor Edward's wife Verity find living in an Elizabethan manor house very romantic – it is far too inconvenient for that. Like Lord and Lady March at Goodwood, Verity Hulse found her children were most affected by the move into Breamore. 'They were eight and eleven when we first came; that was the most difficult time I've had. They just thought they were free and they were so wild for a time that we could never find them in the evening – we could never put them to bed because we never knew where they were!'

Now Verity and Edward Hulse run the house with a small and dedicated staff whose duties are very different from the days when the kitchen's array of copper pans, pestles and mortars were in use, or the eighteenth century beer wagon that used to run up and down the table in the staff hall for them to help themselves. One wonders whether the staff in those days obeyed both the instructions that can be read on each side of the Wagon – 'Waste not, want not', and 'Be charitable to one another'.

The kitchen with the staff beer-barrel on its table-wheels.

The drinking habits of the upper as well as the lower classes left something to be desired in earlier centuries. In the West Drawing Room there is a richly embroidered silk Regency waistcoat that once belonged to the 4th Baronet, Sir Charles Hulse, and still looks exactly as it did the last time he wore it, rather to Lady Hulse's disgust. 'It's very dirty. Dropped drink all down it. It's not been cleaned which I think is terrible. Still there with all the drink down it.'

The 4th Baronet's Regency waistcoat – 'still there with all the drink down it!'

But she did apply her handiwork elsewhere in that room. Sir Westrow, who is a keen amateur picture restorer, had been working on one of the very earliest ever cricketing pictures, 'The Boy with the Bat', painted by William Hoare of Bath around 1760. The young player is holding the two stumps that were in use then, and when Sir Westrow's picture-cleaning became a little too vigorous on the boy's hat Lady Hulse got out the paintbrush and touched it in again. (She was following in an illustrious if not exactly approved tradition, since Sir Winston Churchill is reputed to have touched up some of the portraits at Chequers with his own brush.)

It is surprising that all these rather unusual treasures have survived, since the house has twice been swept by fire, once around 1670 and again rather more damagingly in 1856, but fortunately most of the contents were evacuated in time. It probably helped that Breamore had its own fire engine and fire brigade, right up to as recently as 1920. This was really a necessity since there would have been little chance of a man riding to Salisbury and fetching its Fire Service in time, especially as it was the frequent practice of earlier fire brigades to negotiate their fee while the house was still burning, which

The *Red Rover* stagecoach, prize exhibit of the Carriage Museum.

understandably tended to drive up the price. The fire-equipment can still be seen in the Carriage Museum, together with a gleaming set of phaetons, dog carts, broughams, chaises, horse buses, and the pride of the collection, 'The Red Rover' Stage Coach, which used to run between London and Southampton. It was the last coach that tried to compete with the railways on a regular route up until 1843, from the Bolt-in-Tun in Fleet Street to the Red Lion Inn in Southampton. Edward points out that it used to take eight hours to do the 80 miles, and charged travellers outside tuppence ha'penny a mile at a time when a pint of beer was a penny, which made it more expensive in real terms than first-class travel today.

Walking round the Museums at Breamore one is reminded that the great houses did not exist in a vacuum, they were at the hub of thriving communities of considerable size, and whole families depended for their livelihood on the house and its occupants. In the porch of the Saxon church the name of Captain Edward Hulse who died in action in the First World War is accompanied by other names that recur poignantly again and again, up to the Candy and Witt families who each sent seven members to the carnage in the trenches.

Looking forward as well as back Edward Hulse today is optimistic that Breamore will survive and continue to serve its community. 'I think that in the last ten years the sense of heritage and the necessity to preserve it has simply become something of which the public is aware. One used to find that the Councils as little as twenty years ago opposed conservation procedures and stuck rigidly to the rules. But now they give a tremendous amount of help, most of the media are very sympathetic to Heritage and appreciate that the fantastic amount that we spend on the upkeep of these places actually has to be financed.'

STRATFIELD SAYE

AFTER his victory at Waterloo a grateful nation voted £600,000 to buy the Duke of Wellington a country house; after inspecting several possibilities, including Uppark, he chose Stratfield Saye because of its easy accessibility to the capital. (The house is situated to the west of London in north Hampshire, not far from Reading.) He already owned Apsley House with its famous address, 'Number One, London' (which the 7th Duke presented to the nation in 1947,) so he was not looking for a large, imposing and expensive palace like Blenheim. Several plans were in fact drawn up to build on that grandiose scale across the River Loddon but they never came to anything, and examining the drawings for them in the house one is rather relieved.

His friends were disappointed in his choice. Sir Robert Peel thought the house 'a wretched one, wretchedly furnished' though he conceded that it was 'warm and comfortable'. Those last words are worth keeping in mind when touring the house, as it becomes increasingly apparent that after all those years in the field the Duke went to considerable lengths to ensure his comfort and that of his guests.

He had little enough time to spare from his public duties to supervise a huge building programme, so the alterations he made were not major structural ones, but adaptations and decoration of what already existed in the house when he bought it. Little else was done to Stratfield Saye by his

Design for the great palace that was never built.

88

descendants, until after the Second World War when the 7th Duke decided to reorganize it in memory of his great ancestor as well as a house to live in. This process was continued by his son who inherited in 1972, and who now opens it to the public for a full season every summer. He and his family live here for most of the year, spending some of the rest of their time on their estates in Spain, presented to the Great Duke in gratitude for restoring the Spanish King to his throne.

As the visitor approaches the house down the sweeping avenues it is easy to see why its aspect first attracted the Duke. It is flanked by clumps of impressive woods in the landscaped valley of the Loddon, which is now a winter home to large numbers of wildfowl; and the long straight drive to the front of the house passes through the attractive stable blocks on each side. These were built at the same period as the house, in the seventeenth century, and have the same attractive Dutch gables. The house was painted its warm apricot colour much later.

Present Duke with bust of his ancestor.

Sir William Pitt, Controller of the Household to James I, acquired the estate in 1630 and commissioned the building we see today, and in the eighteenth century, one of his descendants, Lord Rivers, landscaped the park that so appealed to the Duke of Wellington. The Duke added the outer wings that flank the entrance front, and the large conservatory at the back. This subsequently fell into disrepair through neglect, until the present Duke restored it and turned it into a most unusual and attractive swimming pool, where he swims every day when he is in residence. 'We tried to make it in Roman style and I think it's come off quite well really.' This is not an area of the house that members of the public usually see, however. 'They do sometimes see it through the window, but we don't really fancy being the proverbial goldfish in a bowl, so I'm afraid they're not admitted into this part.'

Around the pool are rows of marble columns that were bought in Naples on the recommendation of Lord Elgin (the great marble-collector), for use eventually in the great palace that was going to be built. 'Luckily for me they were shipped from Venice and arrived about 1821 and by that time the

Exterior of the House, framed by the Stable Blocks.

scheme had been abandoned, and they were put into stables and remained there until 1947, when my father unpacked them out of their cases and put them in here.' The busts that stand on the columns were part of the collection of Cardinal Fesch, Napoleon's uncle, which the Duke bought in 1817, and placed in several rooms in the house. Others are to be seen in the Hall, including one of Napoleon as First Consul, but the one that draws the eye is of the Great Duke himself. The profile brings to mind Byron's admiring couplet:

'Proud Wellington, with eagle beak so curled,
That nose, the hook where he suspends the world.'

Bust of the Iron Duke — 'That nose, the hook where he suspends the world'.

From the gallery hang a number of banners. Six of them were designed by Napoleon and the tricolour is embroidered in silver with Imperial bees, the Crown above the 'N' topped by the golden Imperial eagle. He had them made for each Departement of France, and these were surrendered as tribute to the Duke when he entered Paris after Waterloo. They are in such good condition because they were packed away in a box, which was not opened until after the last war by the present Duke's father, who put them on display here. His Garter banner was presented to his son when he died and now has pride of place between the Napoleonic banners. At each end are two plain tricolours; these are the 'rent flags', which are presented each year on the anniversary of Waterloo by the Duke of the day to the Sovereign of the day, as the annual rent for Stratfield Saye. 'These two particular ones were given back on permanent loan to us, one to my father and one to me.'

Hanging in the centre of the Hall is an unusual brass colza-oil lamp designed by Benjamin Wyatt, put in by the 1st Duke. It was still burning oil in World War II, because the 5th Duke was afraid that electricity was a fire-risk. These lamps have been kept in all the reception rooms in the house, but were converted by the present Duke's father to a more modern source of power in 1947. He used to complain that before this everyone had to go to bed at 9.15 because it was so dark, and his son remembers coming to Stratfield Saye on leave in 1944 when 'we sat around in the evening with a Tilly lamp hissing away and candles, and we went up to bed by candlelight.'

The Gallery is supported by what at first glance appear to be granite columns, but tap them and you realise they are made of wood. The head estate painter, George Harding, achieved this elaborate and very convincing disguise in the late 1940s. But something rather more genuine and very much older can be seen inlaid into the flagstones in front of the pillars. The mosaic pavements were excavated by the 2nd Duke in 1866 from the Roman city of Silchester, the site of which is on the property. They bear the marks of much wear from Roman feet, but are now roped off for protection during the season. On a marble table above one of the mosaics stands a large green malachite tazza, a kind of shallow urn, presented to the Great Duke by Tsar Alexander I.

Beyond the columns under the gallery are painted battle scenes which have been grouped by the present Duke, himself a distinguished soldier, to tell the story of some of his ancestors' most famous victories, including the Battle of Vitoria in 1813. Napoleon's brother Joseph, whom he had made King of Spain, was withdrawing to France with a vast amount of baggage and loot. Caught by Wellington's sudden attack Joseph was forced to flee, leaving his booty behind. Among it were many pictures from the Spanish Royal collection which had been cut from their frames and rolled up with manuscripts and state papers. Nobody had time to examine them properly

Page 81. *The Coming of the Storm* by David Teniers the younger.

Top, page 79. The Mexican Feather Fan. *Above*, page 77. The first ethnological paintings, showing the progeny of mixed marriages in Mexico, painted by Murillo's illegitimate son.

Page 103. Copenhagen, who carried the Duke all day at Waterloo.

Page 92. The Hall. Banners right to left – the 7th Duke's Garter Banner, three of Napoleon's Imperial banners, and the annual 'Rent flag' for Stratfield Saye.

Page 89. Present Duke and Duchess in the Lady Charles Room.

and the whole lot was despatched back to England. Some of the canvases were unrolled and used to keep the rain off the pack mules. When their real identity was discovered later Wellington ordered them to be returned to their rightful owner, King Ferdinand VII. But the King knew to whom he owed the restoration of his throne and wished to reward him, 'His Majesty, touched by your delicacy, does not wish to deprive you of that which has come into your possession by means as just as they are honourable.'

The Vitoria pictures at Stratfield Saye have been placed in the main Drawing Room, where they seem to have survived their rough handling by the soldiery and the elements. (The two large and impressive keys formerly kept in that room are the Keys of Madrid, presented to the Duke when he liberated that city from the French in 1812.) Cities and monarchs pressed gifts on him out of relief and gratitude, and many were made specially. In the corridor leading from the Hall to the Drawing Room are cabinets full of beautiful and priceless porcelain, painted often with scenes of his victories, like the set of Meissen presented by the King of Saxony, commemorating his long Peninsular Campaign.

The Dining Room holds reminders of his struggling earlier years and first victories. His formidable mother gazes down from above the doorway. She looks difficult to please, and she certainly despaired of young Arthur, her third son, ever achieving very much. When he did not do very well at Eton she took him away and sent him to the Royal Academy of Equitation at Angers in France. She thought he was 'fit food for powder', and never imagined he would become the greatest soldier of his time. At Angers he

Set of porcelain presented to the 1st Duke in 1818 by Francis I, Emperor of Austria.

The Great Duke's mother, who despaired of him ever succeeding in life.

learnt to speak French well, to ride well, and realised he had found his vocation. To begin with he was overshadowed by his eldest brother, Richard, whose large and imposing portrait hangs over the sideboard. He became Governor-General of India and Marquess Wellesley, and Arthur served under him in India, where he learnt the skills of fighting, often against superior numbers, that led him to much greater victories later on in Europe. His seven years in India are often forgotten today because of his later successes nearer home, but not by his great-great-grandson. 'He went out in command of the 33rd Regiment of Foot, which is now the Duke of Wellington's Regiment, of which I am Colonel-in-Chief, and he progressed to the youngest Major-General in the British Army. He fought a number of very important campaigns, and at the end of the campaign in the Deccan the officers of the Army of India presented him with the Deccan service, sometimes called the Indian plate, which we still use for dinner on important occasions.'

On the sideboard stand two other pieces of gold plate of rather late vintage, coasters on wheels to carry the port round the table, an idea dreamed up by George IV. The bases are inset with medals commemorating various battles in Wellington's campaigns, and they still trundle round the table today as their load gets lighter. In the Music Room there is a picture of the Duke showing the then Prince Regent the field of Waterloo some years after the battle, and ever afterwards he was convinced he had taken part. 'He used to say at the dinner table to the Duke, "Do you remember when I led with Charlie?" And the Duke used to say "Well so Your Majesty's always told me".'

Some well-concealed, more down-to-earth features of the Dining Room are the two panels each side of the doorway which hide behind them two chamber-pots, presumably for diners who did not want to walk some distance to the water-closets, which the Duke was the first to introduce as a domestic convenience. The latter still work, though the elaborate flushing device takes quite a knack to master. The Duke also introduced the first modern central-heating system. Two of the original radiators, huge and not very attractive to our eye, are still in use, and were evidently so unusual then that Queen Victoria complained Stratfield Saye was 'uncomfortably hot'.

All these domestic comforts are thrown into sharp contrast by a look at part of the Duke's campaign-kit which is displayed in the house, and the tableaux of him in the field have been realistically displayed in the Exhibition. In the house are his hearing-aids, his cupping-bowl for being bled, his telescope, compass, and surveying equipment. One of the reasons for his military success was an insistence on surveying the site for a battle himself, and not relying just on subordinates' reports: 'I will get upon my Horse and take a look, and then tell you.' He had learnt from bitter experience early on

The Deccan Dinner Service. *Top* Sir Arthur
Wellesley in India, by John Hoppner.

not to have too high an opinion of the abilities of his brother-officers. 'I have often said that if there were 8 or 10,000 men in Hyde Park, it is not every general that would know how to get them out again.'

There are also a number of his despatches written in the field on donkey-skins. They could be erased and used again, but fortunately for history a few have survived. They reveal his great attention to detail, which allowed him to improvise in emergency and respond quickly to a fast-changing military situation. Napoleon dismissed Wellington as a 'Sepoy general', but although Wellington always had a healthy respect for his adversary he perceived the weakness of French army tactics. 'They planned their campaigns just as you might make a splendid piece of harness. It looks very well, and answers very well, until it gets broken, and then you are done for. Now I made my campaigns of rope. If anything went wrong I tied a knot and went on.'

There are two other intriguing reminders of the Great Duke in the field. One is his campaign service, which was made in Portugal, and is still used for dinner parties by the present Duke and Duchess. The six mugs which fit inside each other for convenience, rather like Russian dolls, are regularly used for picnics. The other reminder is his set of three hinged travelling bookcases which went right round the Peninsula with him.

The present Duke of Wellington is still adding to the mementoes of his ancestor at Stratfield Saye when he can. One of two large hunting pictures in the Music Room was found in Scotland where it had been for a long time. It depicts a meet of the Prince Albert's Harriers in Windsor Great Park. 'It's an important picture for us. I bought it some years ago much to the fury of my trustees, who thought I'd spent much too much money.' Several members of the Wellesley family are shown in attendance on Queen Victoria, including the Marchioness of Douro, who is sitting in the carriage with the Queen, while the 1st Duke and Lord Charles Wellesley, the present Duke's great-grandfather, ride at the wheels.

The 1st Duke's love of reading can be seen in the Library which holds some of Napoleon's books bought by the Duke in Paris when he was Ambassador there after the Emperor's defeat. The swivelling reading-desks were devised by the Duke to take the weight of the heavier books, and he spent a lot of time in this room in later years. Here too is a case holding his batons and sashes as Field-Marshal of Hanover, Prussia, Russia and Britain, Captain-General of Spain, and High Constable of England.

Next to them are two equally treasured locks of hair. One is from the head of George Washington, the other from the mane of Copenhagen, the Duke's famous charger who carried him throughout the Peninsula and all day at Waterloo: 'There may have been many faster horses,' wrote Wellington, 'no doubt many handsomer, but for bottom and endurance I never saw his fellow.' The Music Room which opens off the Library is now largely devoted to the memory of Copenhagen. (The family still has one of his hoofs; there are reputed to be six of these in existence, but the family vouches for the authenticity of this one.) There are several fine pictures of him here, looking very mettlesome, and the troops were always very wary of getting near his hindquarters. He was no respecter of persons and nearly did the Duke himself a serious injury after Waterloo, lashing out when his rider finally dismounted after seventeen hours in the saddle, and then galloping off until he was caught about half a mile away.

But apart from that near-misdemeanour he served his master well, as his great-great-grandson remembers. 'At Quatre Bras on the 16th June he went out to do a reconnaissance on his own, and was very nearly caught by a patrol of French cavalry; had to draw his sword and make a run for it, and as

The Library.

he came up to a line of Highlanders who were kneeling on the ground he said "Keep down but stay where you are and I will clear you", so he cleared the line of British soldiers with Copenhagen.'

The present Duke thinks 'Copenhagen was a marvellous little horse. I was a polo player at one time and I think he would have made a wonderful polo pony. He was only just over 15 hands, very handy'. The 1st Duke brought Copenhagen to Stratfield Saye where he lived out a long retirement, and was finally buried in the paddock with full military honours in 1836. Nearly every small boy who comes here visits Copenhagen's grave, and remembers above all the stories that prompted the inscription on his headstone:

'God's humble instrument, though meaner clay,
Shall share the glory of that glorious day.'

Copenhagen's hoof, and some of the Duke's campaign-kit.

103

The price of victory on that glorious day was a very high one, as the Duke told Creevey in Brussels immediately afterwards. 'It has been a damned serious business, Blucher and I have lost 30,000 men. It has been a damned nice thing – the nearest run thing you ever saw in your life'. Most of us were taught at school a slightly different and shorter version of that quotation of the Iron Duke's, but we seem to have been misled about other statements made on that day. When General Cambronne, Commander of Napoleon's Old Guard, was invited to surrender he exclaimed, 'Merde', which has been sometimes translated by historians as 'The Guard dies but never surrenders'.

Wellington and Napoleon were born the same year, 1769, and although their names will always be coupled together they never actually met, and only faced one another on the same battlefield once, the final one. Although it crowned Wellington's military career, the cost in casualties was massive. His first rough estimate of 30,000 was too high, but the final count of British and Prussians was around 22,000, and the French casualties were over 25,000.

The present Duke has visited Waterloo several times and it is not surprising that he still finds it a deeply moving experience. He clearly identifies with the emotions of that day: 'As he rode back across the battlefield he was in a mood of deep depression. He sat down at dinner at his headquarters where he was accustomed to dining with his staff, and all the places at the table were empty, except for his Spanish A.D.C., Alava. The whole lot had been killed or wounded. And he turned to Alava and said "The finger of God was upon me this day Alava".'

His favourite A.D.C., Alexander Gordon, lay dying in Wellington's own bed, so he put a pallet on the ground and fell into an exhausted sleep. When Dr Hume woke him at about three in the morning to tell him Gordon had just died, he asked for the list of casualties that had come in since midnight. As he recited the names, Hume felt the tears fall on his hand. 'Well thank God I don't know what it is to lose a battle, but certainly nothing can be more painful than to gain one with the loss of so many of one's friends.' That poignant tableau can be seen in the Exhibition, as the Duke sat up writing his despatches for England in the company of his dead friend.

Although soldiering was his life he was hugely relieved the Wars were over. As he said to Lady Shelley, 'I hope to God that I have fought my last battle, it is a bad thing to be always fighting.' The long and often wearisome struggle for mastery of Europe made the Duke philosophical about the fame he had achieved, especially with the cheering crowds who greeted his return from Waterloo. Asked if he were not pleased to be so enthusiastically mobbed he rather caustically replied, 'Not in the least, if I had failed they would have shot me.' Indeed, the London mob broke his windows at Apsley House much later because of his opposition to the Great Reform Bill.

But he remained for most people a figure of admiration and wonderment, enhanced by his crispness of speech. When Lady Salisbury asked him if he never lay awake with anxiety he simply said, 'It does no good. I make it a point never to lie awake.'

When the French reviewer of the Duke's *Despatches* complained of finding 'duty' on every page and 'glory' never, the Duke riposted, 'That is the difference between the French and the English soldiers; with the French glory is the cause; with us, the result.'

It may be that he bought items from the Cardinal Fesch collection with all its Bonapartist grandeur as a reminder that the search for glory can lead to your downfall. The bust of Napoleon as a Roman Emperor stands on a plinth in the Gallery near one of Massena, one of his ablest Generals who met defeat at the hands of Wellington in the Peninsula. But the Gallery also celebrates the arts of peace, and the walls are rather unusually covered with prints, many of them Shakespearean scenes, stuck straight on to the walls and gilded. The Duke was so taken with the effect that he repeated it in some of the smaller rooms downstairs and several of the bedrooms upstairs. The yellow, blue and brown carpet that runs the length of the Gallery was specially designed for this room by the present Duke's father, and woven at the Spanish Royal Carpet Factory in Madrid in 1952.

In the Small Drawing Room at the end of the Gallery is a picture of the Duke in the last year of his life, with four of his five grandchildren. He cannot have awed children like he did most of the adult population, since he was often caught having pillow-fights with them, even when he became Prime Minister in 1828. We usually think of him as a stern, hard man, who flogged his troops and described them once as 'the scum of the earth', but one witness of his sense of humour said he had 'the laugh of a horse with whooping cough'.

His achievements and offices in British domestic politics are not remembered with the same admiration as his European exploits, but he does have the historical distinction of being the last Prime Minister to fight a duel in office, against Lord Winchelsea, though neither man was injured. He carried into civilian life his firm belief in discipline and order, which he saw threatened by the Radical leaders whipping up the unrest of the people in the often turbulent post-War years. When the great Whig Duke of Bedford, owner of the fabulous wealth of Woburn, said the nation's choice was now between anarchy and despotism and he preferred anarchy, Wellington's comment was cutting: 'I can tell Johnny Bedford if we have anarchy, I'll have Woburn.'

Often dismissive of the great he could be compassionate with the humble. When one of his gamekeepers was shot dead by a poacher he stopped rearing game, since all the pheasants in the world were not worth one human life,

Bust of Napoleon as a Roman Emperor, in the Gallery.
The Gallery.

though now the approaches to Stratfield Saye are alive with pheasants, and the present Duke is a very keen shot. He and the Duchess like to walk in the woods with their little dog, Napoleon. They are dominated by the towering 'Wellingtonias', the *Sequoiadendron giganteas* which were first discovered the year after the Great Duke's death and named after him. His name, and that of his last battle, have been given to streets, bridges, barracks, colleges, public houses, railway stations, and of course boots, and because he lived to the great age of 83 few people could remember a time when he did not tower over his countrymen. This was perhaps articulated best by Prince Albert's secretary when the Duke died at Walmer Castle on September 14th, 1852. He sent the news to the Royal Family at Balmoral, 'The greatest man that ever England knew is no more, one can hardly realise to oneself the idea of England without the Duke of Wellington.' The Queen and Prince Consort decided to postpone the funeral until after Parliament met in November so that 'every Englishman shall have time and opportunity to take his humble part in it'.

The 'Wellingtonias',
*Sequoiadendron
Gigantea.*

Prince Albert took personal charge of the arrangements for the State Funeral, the first for someone not of royal descent, and an honour only conferred on one other occasion, 112 years later, for that other great war leader, Winston Churchill. He instructed the Department of Practical Art, which he had recently set up, to design a suitable 'Triumphal Car' for the Funeral, and supervised the design himself. It can now be seen in a large barn at Stratfield Saye, where it was brought in 1981 from the Crypt at St Paul's. Made from melted down cannons captured at Waterloo, it carries the names of the Duke's victories in India and Europe, and battle trophies of weapons, cuirasses, helmets, colours and standards. 21 feet long, 12 feet wide, it weighed 18 tons, and was pulled by twelve black dray horses. Its height was limited to 17 feet to get it under Temple Bar, but it proved to be as unwieldy as it looks, and stuck several times on its way to St Paul's.

The Funeral Car, made to Prince Albert's orders.

Over a million people watched it pass, and one writer thought that the sight of all the hats raised looked like 'the sudden rising from the ground and settling again of a huge flock of birds'. The present Duke has had an engraving of the scene as the Car passes Apsley House blown up into a huge panorama, to give the visitor an idea of the scale and atmosphere of this sombre event. There is another rather touching link from that time to this. The Car was decorated with wreaths, from one of which a sprig of cypress was plucked, rooted and grew into a great tree. In 1953 Lady Jane Wellesley, the young daughter of the present Duke, took a cutting from this tree and planted it in the grounds here. Today it too has grown into a tall cypress, a living memorial to the greatest Englishman of his time.

PENSHURST PLACE

SET among the hills of Kent some five miles from Tonbridge, Penshurst Place is the ancestral home of Viscount De L'Isle V.C., K.G. In its time it has been owned by two kings, four dukes, and a great merchant prince, but since 1552 it has been the home of the Sidney family. In the eighteenth century one overwhelmed visitor wrote 'I know not any family that for arts and arms, greatness of courage, and nobility of mind, have excelled the Sidney race'. A century later, another asserted that the house 'has been the natal home of poetry, romance, patriotism, the theatre of sumptuous hospitality, the abode of chivalry, and the resting place of virtue and honour'.

In the steps of that tradition it seems appropriate that the present owner should have won the highest decoration for bravery in time of war (he was awarded the Victoria Cross for his part in the Battle of Anzio in 1944); and held high office in times of peace (especially as Governor General of Australia from 1961–65). Lord De L'Isle has devoted himself to repairing the damage done to his home by German bombing in the last war, and is very keen to see that the varied history of Penshurst is better-known. Naturally he is particularly proud of his own family, the Sidneys, but he is just as interested in the history and achievements of earlier occupants.

The house embraces the architectural styles of more different periods than any other in this book, and owes its character more to the taste and personality of its owners than to that of its architects. Wings have been thrown out to produce a shape that now resembles the letter 'H' with an extra arm; as the visitors move from one to the next they pass from one century into another. But the dominant atmosphere remains that of the earliest part of the building, which dates back to the fourteenth century.

The best approach is from the south, through the formal garden, pausing by the fountain to study the long facade of local sandstone, built with blocks of different size and colour, some of them streaked with brownish stains of iron. In the sunshine the whole building is a glowing golden colour.

The name Penshurst comes from its thirteenth century owner Sir Stephen de Penchester. Constable of Dover Castle and Warden of the Cinque Ports, his main residence was at Allington Castle near Maidstone and all that survives him here is his name. The man who established Penshurst in its earliest glory was Sir John de Pulteney, a rich merchant who bought the estate in 1338. He built the great Barons Hall, so imposing that it is believed to be the work of the King's carpenter, William Hurley. Its dimensions are impressive, 62 feet by 39 feet, with a magnificent chestnut-beamed roof that rises above 60 feet at its apex; but it is the ingenious construction of this huge space that excites admiration six centuries later. The system of king-posts resting on collar-beams and arched braces allowed Hurley to insert windows high up in the arches as well as in the walls, so that the Hall is flooded with light. In times of revelry a huge central fire was lit on the octagonal fireplace, a most unusual feature for a hall of this size. Lord De L'Isle still lights the fire in the hall on special occasions, such as his younger daughter's wedding. 'It works,' he says. 'The smoke goes out through the tiles.'

The cost of such an undertaking even then must have been prodigious, but Pulteney was a particularly successful businessman and banker. He used his fortunes made in the wool and wine trades to lend money to Edward III to finance the French wars. Peacetime Crown revenues were less than £40,000 a year, but by 1337 Edward had promised more than three times that

Exterior, south front.

The 14th Century Barons Hall. Henry VIII dined here.

amount to his continental allies, so he borrowed £200,000 free of interest from a group of wool merchants led by Pulteney, in return for granting them a monopoly in the export of wool. Pulteney became a royal agent in both commercial and state affairs, but he soon learnt that monarchs do not relish being beholden to too powerful subjects. He and other financiers were arrested by the King in 1340 for fraudulent practices. Lord De L'Isle thinks he may have put him in prison 'just to teach him a lesson . . . quite a way of teaching bankers'.

These were insecure times for most people, but especially in Kent. The upheavals of the Peasants' Revolt and the French raids on the coast in the fourteenth century led to defensive measures being taken at Penshurst.

112

Towers were built and crenellated walls were thrown out (though the latter feature was prized for ornamentation as much as defence). However the only tower to survive in its original state is the one the visitor walks through between the garden and the south entrance to the Barons Hall.

The greatest threat to the masters of Penshurst usually came from the Crown. It was briefly owned in succession by Henry V's younger brothers, the Duke of Bedford and the Duke of Gloucester; on the latter's death it was granted by Henry VI to the 1st Duke of Buckingham. He and his two heirs all came to violent ends. The 2nd Duke entertained Edward IV here, but his real rise to power came when he helped Richard III to the throne. When he turned against the King he was betrayed, beheaded and his estate confiscated. Henry VII reversed the attainder and restored the property to Edward, 3rd Duke of Buckingham. It was he who entertained his King, Henry VIII, at Penshurst in 1519, with a lavishness that proved his downfall. It is easy to imagine Henry VIII dining on the dais at one end of the Hall, although Lord De L'Isle does not think he quite behaved in the way Charles Laughton portrayed him on screen in the thirties: 'I think he did wash his hands, and I don't think he chucked chicken bones over his shoulder!' The occasion in the Barons Hall cost Buckingham over £2,300, an enormous sum for those days. He clearly failed to see the dangers of trying to match the King's magnificence, and over-reached himself at the Field of the Cloth of Gold, Henry VIII's showy summit meeting with Francis I of France, by appearing with the royal quarterings of England on his arm. Shortly afterwards Henry charged him with treason, tried him by Star Chamber, and he went to the block like his father. Penshurst reverted to the Crown again, but Henry seems to have done little to it except extend the park for hunting.

It was his son, Edward VI, who granted it in 1552 to his tutor and steward of his household, Sir William Sidney, in whose family it has remained ever since. He died two years later, passing the estate to his son Sir Henry, who was the young King's closest companion. The Royal portrait hangs above the door into the Long Gallery, near that of his more famous sister, Queen Elizabeth I. Around them Lord De L'Isle has grouped pictures of those Sidneys who enjoyed their royal favour. The many portraits in the Long Gallery help to bring the family history to life. As Lord De L'Isle explains, 'We rearranged them when we came here to give a logical sequence.'

Sir Henry united the Sidneys with the Dudley line when he married Mary Dudley in 1551. He served the Crown in Ireland and Wales with a devotion to duty that was rather taken for granted by his Queen, who could be rather mean in financial matters, making her greater lavishness with honours a mixed blessing. When it looked as if he was about to be raised to the peerage he had to ask Burghley to prevent it, as he felt he could not afford to sustain the title properly. It must have been this conscientious approach to duty that

Edward VI, who died in the arms of Henry Sidney.

Queen Elizabeth I.

led Holinshed to extol him as the paragon of the Court, 'for comeliness of person, gallantness and liveliness of spirit, virtue, quality, beauty and good composition of body'.

His brother-in-law Robert Dudley, Earl of Leicester, was one of the Queen's favourites although, or perhaps because, he was much less virtuous. In fact Lord De L'Isle thinks 'he was really rather a bounder'. He died without any legitimate heirs so his estate and later his titles passed to his nephew Sir Robert Sidney. Leicester's great Sword of State is one of the prized possessions to be seen at Penshurst.

It was Robert who built the Long Gallery in 1599, at a cost of less than £600. It is beautifully light and airy, with windows in each long side and one end; understandably it is Lord De L'Isle's favourite room in the house. It fits the description in *Arcadia*, the greatest work of Robert's famous brother, the soldier-poet Sir Philip Sidney: 'Built of fair and strong stone, not affecting so much any extraordinary kind of fineness as an honourable representing of a firm stateliness; each place handsome without curiosity and homely without loathsomeness, all more lasting than beautiful.' Philip did in fact inherit Penshurst from his father, but died only a few months afterwards from wounds received at the Battle of Zutphen in 1586, fighting with the Dutch in their struggle against Spanish rule. Soldier, courtier and poet, his life blazed

Robert Dudley, Earl of Leicester. *Right* Lord De L'Isle demonstrates the size and weight of the Sword of State that the Earl of Leicester carried before Elizabeth I.

The Long Gallery – Lord De L'Isle's favourite room.

briefly like a shooting-star, and he was mourned as 'the glory of the family, the hope of mankind, the most lively pattern of virtue and the delight of the learned world'. Elizabeth I took the unusual step of allowing him a state funeral, though as Lord De L'Isle remarks, 'She wasn't so nice to him when he was alive ... he never received any order of decoration.' Sir Philip Sidney's intelligence and sensitivity shine out of his portrait, hanging in the Long Gallery next to that of his beloved sister Mary, Countess of Pembroke and mistress of Wilton, where Philip actually wrote most of *Arcadia*.

Another family group can be seen in the Solar Room above the Barons Hall, in a large 'conversation-piece', a very early example of a group portrait. The picture shows Barbara, wife of Robert Sidney, with six of their children. Next to it stands her husband in solitary splendour. Now wealthy enough to accept the peerage his father had had to refuse, he appears as Lord Lisle, in his robes of office, which his descendant says are 'the sort of robes that we still wear'.

The Solar Room was originally a withdrawing-room for the ladies of the household, with a peephole (which still exists), enabling them to look down into the Barons Hall on the menfolk feasting and drinking. Robert moved

1st Lord Lisle.

Barbara Gamage, wife of Robert Sidney, 1st Lord Lisle.

that activity upstairs, and the Solar has become the Dining Room, still used on great occasions and family reunions at Christmas. The Great Hall is now used for functions much more rarely.

Robert's fortunes flourished under James I. His uncle's title, the Earldom of Leicester, which had died with him, was revived and conferred on him as the Dudley heir through his mother. It is difficult to disentangle the work done at Penshurst by Robert from that of his father, but between them they are responsible for the happy merging with previous centuries; unlike the building of most of their contemporaries, whose tendency was to demolish and start again in their search for a lasting memorial in brick or stone.

Fashions change in more than architecture of course. In 1911 *Country Life* was lamenting that the country houses found it difficult to keep their servants, in contrast to those earlier days when 'the servants from Kent will not stay in London above three days and then they steal home again'. Their employers too were not anxious to spend time away from home. On one of Robert's rare trips abroad, his steward Rowland Whyte reported, 'My Lady takes great pleasure in this place, and surely I never saw a sweeter. All things finely prospering about it. The garden is well kept.'

The troubled Stuart times cast their shadow over Penshurst as they did over so many of the great houses of England. Both sons of the 2nd Earl of Leicester took the Parliamentary side, and both were appointed judges at the trial of Charles I. They were spared the consequences, however, since in the event, Philip did not serve, and the younger, Algernon, managed to avoid signing the judgement. Lord De L'Isle believes that caution and realism must have been a family trait. 'During the Commonwealth their father, the 2nd Earl of Leicester, lived here and sat rather carefully on the fence; until the Protector sent his agents to say if he didn't sign an oath of allegiance he couldn't sue his tenants for their rents. So he signed.'

The Dining Room, also known as the Solar Room.

Penshurst survived both the anti-Royalist purges of the Commonwealth and the swing of the pendulum at the Restoration of Charles II, at least for a while. This period is captured at the other end of the Long Gallery, with an interesting if rather gloomy picture of Philip, 3rd Earl of Leicester, and his two brothers. Algernon remained a pronounced Republican, and Lord De L'Isle does not admire his politics, but he does commend his courage: 'I always think his picture gives him adenoids, and he had his head cut off for allegedly taking part in the Rye House Plot to murder Charles II.' Algernon's bones lie in the family vault, but not his head, which presumably rests somewhere in the Tower of London. Before the execution in 1683, friends urged him to beg the King to let his family have his body for burial, but obdurate to the last, he replied in rather less than courtly language, 'Go tell His Majesty he can make a snuffbox of my arse if he listeth.' The youngest brother Robert in the same picture had a rather different connection with the Merry Monarch. 'He was rather a naughty boy,' says Lord De L'Isle. 'He was known as Le Beau Sidney, and he was the lover of Lucy Walters before King Charles II.'

Their sister Dorothy appears next to them as a shepherdess. Her beauty was captured in paint by many other eager artists, and most famously in print by the poet Waller, who courted her unsuccessfully. The depth of his passion still speaks to us in his poem which begins with his pet-name for her, 'Sacharissa':

> 'Her presence has such more than human grace,
> That it can civilise the rudest place.
> And beauty too, and order, can impart,
> Where nature ne'er intended it, nor art.'

But the sorrow of his unrequited love he put into his song:

> 'Go, lovely Rose –
> Tell her that wastes her time and me
> That now she knows,
> When I resemble her to thee,
> How sweet and fair she seems to be.'

Dorothy married Lord Spencer in 1639, a choice which cannot have pleased her brothers since he was a strong Royalist who fought for the King and was killed in 1643 at the Battle of Newbury; however she then spent the first seven years of her widowhood at Penshurst.

Perhaps because the family was so divided by the struggle between Crown and Parliament there are not the great profusion of Stuart likenesses here that are so popular in so many noble houses. The most striking sight that dates from the period of Charles II is the huge silver wine cistern and cooler

119

Top left The three Sidney brothers, Philip, Algernon and Robert. Their expressions seem to foretell their rather unhappy fates. *Above* The Charles II wine fountain in the Dining Room. *Left* Lady Dorothy Sidney, 1617–1684, as a shepherdess. Her beauty was immortalised by the poet Waller.

that now stands in the Dining Room, and this is only a recent arrival. It was given to Lord De L'Isle's first wife by her uncle, who was a great collector of silver *objets d'art*.

In the eighteenth century the family line began to zigzag. The 4th Earl of Leicester's three sons all died without legitimate heirs and in 1743 that title became extinct. The main estate went to Elizabeth Sidney, grand-daughter of the 4th Earl, the 'ample lady in strawberry pink' in the large family portrait that dominates Queen Elizabeth's Drawing Room. She was married to William Perry, who was granted royal licence to use the name and arms of Sidney. Lord De L'Isle describes him as a 'rather grotesque little man', an opinion echoing his contemporaries and reflected in the same portrait. Only one of the daughters in the picture survived him. He made many changes at Penshurst, introducing sash windows all over the place, but they were so insensitively out of keeping that they have now been removed. He put Venetian windows into the Long Gallery and bought a large number of rather inferior Italian pictures, all since sold.

Horace Walpole recorded the scene then in typical waspish style: 'This morning we have been to Penshurst – but oh! how fallen! The apartments are the grandest I have seen in any of these old palaces, but furnished in a tawdry modern taste. There are loads of portraits; but most of them seem christened by chance, like children at a foundling hospital.'

Lord De L'Isle recounts that on one occasion Walpole actually 'barged his way into Mr Perry's dressing room – and then commented that Mr Perry was rather annoyed.' In this case, Lord De L'Isle is on the side of his ancestor – who he says was 'amiable', even if his taste was misguided. However, Perry's capricious changes were brought to an end when a jury certified him as 'a lunatic with lucid intervals but insufficient to govern himself or his property', and he died in an asylum in 1757.

His wife outlived him by 26 years, and was succeeded in 1783 by John Shelley Sidney, son of her eldest daughter Elizabeth and Bysshe Shelley, grandfather of the poet Percy Bysshe Shelley, by his first marriage. Although Lord De L'Isle has the poet's baronetcy and he and his son are the only male Shelleys left, he reports that 'neither of us write poetry'.

During his minority John Shelley Sidney's trustees allowed the estate to run down, driving one visitor to predict the worst. 'The mansion is now deserted; and will probably before another generation passes be known only as a ruin … the gardens still retain their original form of terraces, and multiplied divisions, but they are neglected, and indeed form a perfect wilderness.' But soon after Waterloo John Shelley Sidney set about a large programme of restoration, employing the architect, John Biagio Rebecca. His exteriors, though not inspiring, are in keeping with the rest of the Tudor extension. The sandstone of Rebecca's North Front is a rather pallid grey, in sharp contrast to the tints of the South Front. But his real gift was for interiors where he had a delicate light touch, and a consistency of approach that adapted Gothic details to rooms of classical proportions.

The bulk of his work was the repair and redecoration of the private apartments in the west and north wings, and one of his most striking innovations was the vaulted corridor he built to join them to the State rooms. The transition is sudden and startling. The entrance to Rebecca's wing is from the dais in the Barons Hall, so with one pace you leave the fourteenth century and step into the nineteenth. Indeed the first sight is of the twentieth, as Lord De L'Isle's large collection of hats for all occasions sits on the hall table. Traversing the corridor brings you to the Vestibule and another connection with the Crown.

The Duke of Clarence was the third son of George III and never expected to ascend the throne himself. His naval career was frustrated rather than helped by his princely status, and the Royal Marriages Act made it difficult for him to have a wife of his own choosing. So he took as his mistress the beautiful and talented comic actress Mrs Jordan, and pictures of the two of them in their youth hang together in one corner of the Vestibule. 'Mistress' conveys an inappropriate impression of a fleeting secret relationship, when in fact their union was known and recognised by all, lasting twenty years and producing ten children. As Lord De L'Isle explains, 'They lived at Bushey together and she entertained for him and was perfectly respectable.'

Their eldest daughter Sophia married Philip Sidney, son of John Shelley Sidney. Illegitimacy rarely seems to have been a bar to advancement if the father was Royal; and when the Duke finally and rather unexpectedly succeeded to the throne as William IV, he did not forget his first family. Although he had now married, he and Queen Adelaide frequently entertained Sophia and her husband at Windsor. In those pre-Victorian days sexual indiscretion did not carry the moral stigma it acquired later, and the tone was set by Royalty. When William's brother, the Duke of Cambridge, heard the Ten Commandments read in Church one Sunday and the clergyman reached 'Thou shalt not commit Adultery' he was heard to exclaim quite audibly 'Damn! Now I remember where I left my umbrella!'

Sophia was the King's favourite daughter and in 1835 she persuaded him to make her husband the first Baron De L'Isle and Dudley. He showered other gifts on the two, including a magnificent set of porcelain bearing his crest, the initial 'W', and the orders of chivalry of Britain and Hanover. This is displayed in cabinets, but is rarely used today as it is irreplaceable. The Vestibule also contains a full-length portrait of King William wearing Naval uniform.

The restoration of Penshurst continued throughout the nineteenth century. The style begun by Rebecca was continued by Devey, who took out

Above The Rockingham Service presented by William IV to Philip Sidney after his marriage to the King's illegitimate daughter, Sophia.

Right William IV in Naval uniform.

William Perry's sash-windows, and then by Crace, whose most impressive room is the Library. It has undergone several transformations. Originally built in about 1575 as a loggia, it became a cloister, then it was glazed, then it was turned into a library, and at one stage in the last century it doubled as a billiard-room.

The present Viscount also inherited by a kind of lateral succession, as the younger child of a youngest son, but he was by chance well-trained for the task, as he became a chartered accountant in the thirties. It has taken five generations to put Penshurst back into habitable repair, and surveying their work as well as the earlier changes he has formed his 'conjugal theory of architecture, when a family lives in a house for a long time over the generations. When an heir succeeds his wife says to him "darling I'm not going to live in your old dump unless you make it properly modernised". And that is the history of this house.'

It is certainly borne out by his own experience. His first wife refused to move to Penshurst after the war until he had asked the agent to test the drains. 'I went home one day to see him and there was a little party digging a trench across the lawn, so I asked what they were doing and was told they were trying to find the main drain. It had completely disappeared. It had fractured and the gravel under the lawn had sunk, and the pipes had just disintegrated. So my wife was right and we renewed the main drain, though it seemed a perfectly good sewerage system to me, the lawn would have been greener.'

And in more recent years the theory still holds true. The present Lady De L'Isle has played a major part in restoring the private apartments in the Victorian wing, singling out the drawing room for special attention. 'As it hadn't been painted for probably 100 years, we thought it would be nice to have one really gay and bright room,' she explained. 'We took all the furniture out of it on a freezing cold day and sat on the radiator and wondered what colour to choose.'

The drawing room features a strikingly joyful Elizabethan painting over the fireplace. Although Lord and Lady De L'Isle are only too happy to share their home and all the beautiful and historic artefacts in it with the public, Lady De L'Isle explained that 'it seemed sad not to live with *any* of the pictures on the private side of the house. So we rather bravely decided to take it out of the State rooms.' The painting, by an unknown French artist, shows Queen Elizabeth I executing the final figure of a dance called La Volta with Lord Leicester. It is, as Lord De L'Isle points out, a highly political picture, which 'pours cold water on the idea that the Queen should marry the Duc d'Alençon', who is depicted in a somewhat compromising pose with his arm round a serving maid.

When Lord De L'Isle inherited Penshurst in 1945, German flying bombs had damaged roofs and shattered windows, letting in the cold and damp to furniture and pictures. Essential repairs took several years before he could take up the work of restoration where his forebears had left off. He admits that at times coping with the rambling house has been an uphill struggle: 'Sometimes my family find it a bit oppressive.' But he has ridden out some of the storms by following the encouraging advice of a distinguished visitor, who once told him, 'Don't despair, feed on a policy of little hopes.' Some of these hopes, little and not so little, have indeed been fulfilled. One feels that if Ben Jonson revisited it now the lines he wrote in 1616 would still be fitting:

> 'Thou art not, Penshurst, built to envious show
> Of touch or marble, nor canst boast a row
> Of polished pillars, or a roof of gold;
> Thou hast no lanthorn, whereof tales are told
> On stairs, or courts, but standest an ancient pile,
> And these grudged at, art reverenced the while.'

Exterior, the West Wing.

Part of Penshurst's appeal is the sense of history unfolding that its 'hotch-potch' of architectural styles gives the visitor. The house has been in the hands of the same family for five centuries, and has welcomed a stream of visitors over the years, ever since Tunbridge Wells became a spa in the eighteenth century and the gentry came here on afternoons out, tipping the porter a guinea for showing them round. Now it is open to visitors throughout the spring and summer, and is frequently hired as a backdrop for a wide variety of films, which by careful selection of angles can represent very different periods in history. In any event, Lord De L'Isle is keen to share his inheritance: 'If we lived here in an empty house, because there's very few people in it, I think one would feel awful.' Above all he is anxious that it should not become a museum; he wants to preserve its present very strong family atmosphere which makes its six centuries of history a living thing.

WILTON

WILTON has been the family seat of the Earls of Pembroke since the middle of the sixteenth century, passing in an unbroken line from father to son, or brother to brother, right down to the 17th Earl, who inherited the titles and estates in 1969. He is perhaps better known as the television director Henry Herbert, with a particular interest in historical and literary dramas on such subjects as the Civil War or more recently, Oscar Wilde, which he filmed in the setting of Wilton. In this he is carrying on the family tradition, since the house has attracted writers, painters and scholars in addition to royal and noble visitors ever since it was first built.

The town of Wilton was the ancient capital of the Saxon kingdom of Wessex, and King Egbert founded a priory of Benedictine nuns nearby in the eighth century, which eventually became an abbey of great wealth and size.

The present (or 17th) Earl of Pembroke at Wilton.

However, the only relic of that time to be seen today is in the old fourteenth century 'Bell-House' in the grounds. Everything else was swept away by Sir William Herbert, the founder of the family fortunes and the first Herbert to live here.

His story began inauspiciously, when he was forced to flee the country after killing a man in a drunken brawl. But he redeemed himself by serving the French king, Francis I, with such courage in battle and wit at Court, that Francis wrote on his behalf to his brother-monarch, Henry VIII.

After a brief exile he returned to England and in 1534 married Anne Parr. Her marriage dowry was small – she and her sister Katherine had had only £800 settled on the two of them for this purpose – but if he chose his wife for love and not position he gained the latter too by the most enormous stroke of luck. Nine years later his sister-in-law, the twice-widowed Katherine, became the sixth and last wife of Henry VIII. William Herbert was already close enough to the King to have been granted a coat of arms and crest (now proudly exhibited over the front door of Wilton House), but the year after his wedding to Katherine, the King gave his young brother-in-law the lands of the dissolved Abbey of Wilton.

Sir William wasted no time and the house he built was finished about 1550. Royal favour did not die with Henry in 1547, for he had nominated Sir William Herbert to be one of the young Edward VI's Privy Council of twelve. Throughout the troubled intrigues of Edward VI's and Mary Tudor's reigns, Sir William managed (literally) to keep his head, evincing a political skill and judgment that his heirs were to show time and again in later conflicts and national upheavals.

When the pendulum swung in his favour with Mary's death and Elizabeth's accession in 1558, Pembroke hastened to accompany her progress into London, and soon he was in high favour with the fourth monarch he served. She frequently dined with him at his London home on the Thames, Baynard's Castle, but it was his son rather than he who was granted the expensive 'honour' of entertaining her and her retinue at Wilton, during her royal progresses around the country. This may have been because of her great displeasure at one of his father's rare mistakes of judgment, when he supported the Duke of Norfolk's fatal attempt to marry Mary, Queen of Scots. Norfolk lost his head, and Pembroke was lucky to get off with a tongue-lashing from the Queen. When he protested that his support for the match did not mean he was disloyal to Elizabeth she told him curtly that he spoke like a fool of a soldier and knew not what he was saying.

He returned to Wilton to escape her wrath, which had fortunately long-cooled by the year of his death in 1579. He bequeathed to his son Henry a great and wealthy estate with a large household – when the Queen came to stay for three nights in 1574 the Earl was able to muster 210 men in livery to

Page 124. Queen Elizabeth
dancing La Volta, with Robert
Dudley, Earl of Leicester.

Page 121. William Perry and his
wife Elizabeth Sidney with
some of their children (detail).

Page 142. The Palladian Bridge, view from the House.

Page 138. The ceiling of the Double Cube, and the 17 ft family portrait.

Page 133. The Single Cube.

Top, page 149. Exterior, South front. *Above*, page 157. The Prince of Wales' 'old bed'. *Right*, page 157. The Uppark Cup, topped with the Prince of Wales' feathers.

Page 156 Sir Harry Fetherstonhaugh as a young man of 22, by Batoni.

welcome her. However, very little of the Tudor house she visited has survived, apart from the central tower on the east front which used to be the main entrance, and the central courtyard which the existing house still surrounds.

The 2nd Earl was highly favoured by his Queen, and she bestowed many lucrative honours on him. His first two marriages ended in annulment and death respectively, and neither produced children, but in 1577 he married Mary, daughter of Sir Henry Sidney of Penshurst and sister of the great poet Sir Philip Sidney. Mary was still only in her mid-teens, while her husband was in his early forties, but they seem to have been an ideally-matched couple, becoming great patrons of the stage and of literature. She outlived her husband by twenty years which may be why she is remembered more than he, especially through the pen of the historian John Aubrey: 'In her time Wilton House was like a college, there were so many learned and ingeniose persons. She was the greatest patronesse of wit and learning of any lady of her time.'

Her love of literature must have been bound up with her devotion to her elder brother Philip, who came to stay with her at Wilton in 1580 when he was rather out of favour at Court, for writing to the Queen about the dismay of many of her subjects at the possibility of her marrying the French Duke of Alençon in terms more direct than was normally wise to use. Elizabeth's loss benefited not just Wilton but posterity, for during that time he wrote *The Countess of Pembroke's Arcadia*, to entertain his sister during her first pregnancy, and dedicated the work to her. In later years the Single Cube Room was decorated with panels showing scenes from *Arcadia*, and what the author dismissed as 'this idle work of mine' proved to be one of the most popular works of fiction of the English Renaissance. Mary's tribute to her brother's memory was to supervise the publication of his three major works, the *Arcadia*, *Astrophel and Stella*, and the *Apologie for Poetrie*, and it was her efforts that brought them to the public at large.

Many other writers were drawn to Wilton by her encouragement, including Philip Massinger, Ben Jonson and Edmund Spenser. At the turn of the seventeenth century, not long after the death of her husband, Shakespeare himself came here, and his company gave the first performance of *As You Like It*, or possibly *Twelfth Night*, as both plays have been mentioned in different accounts. In memory of that visit an attractive statue of the Bard was commissioned in the eighteenth century, which now stands in the Front Hall. (Designed by William Kent and sculpted by Scheemakers in 1743, it cost the 9th Earl the sum of £100.18s.4¼d.) Mary's son William Herbert is thought by some to be the 'Mr W.H.' of the sonnets, but that too is a matter of some dispute. What is not, however, is that Shakespeare dedicated the First Folio of his works in 1623 'to the most noble and incomparable paire of brethren William, Earl of Pembroke and Lord Chamberlain to the King's most excellent Majestie, and Philip, Earl of Montgomery, Gentleman of His Majestie's Bedchamber'.

Both brothers played important roles in the life of the country as well as in the transformation of Wilton into its present magnificence. In William's case his legacy to Wilton is rather surprising. As a young man he only wanted to sparkle at Court, but his dalliance with Mary Fitton, one of the Queen's maids of honour, made her pregnant, and when he refused to marry her the Queen flung him into the Fleet prison and then banished him from Court. This was the greatest punishment of all: 'I have not yet been a day in the

William Shakespeare, by Scheemakers.

country, and I am as weary of it as if I had been a prisoner there seven year.' He pleaded through Sir Robert Cecil for Royal permission to go abroad, and when it was finally granted he set off for Italy accompanied by a young man of 28 called Inigo Jones, the foundation of a family connection with the great architect that came to its peak of fruition under his brother Philip, the 4th Earl.

William's extravagant tastes necessitated marriage to a rich heiress, and he settled for 'the dwarfish and unattractive' daughter of the Earl of Shrewsbury, Lady Mary Talbot, but seems to have continued indulging his affections for the opposite sex. At the same time he and especially his brother Philip soon became favourites to the new king, James I, who had a pronounced weakness for well-favoured young men. The Van Dyck portraits of the two brothers holding their wands of office, as Lord Steward and Lord Chamberlain, hang each side of the fireplace in the Double Cube Room at Wilton, both looking confident and imperious, as they had a right to do in their favoured position. The present Earl believes that Shakespeare's dedica-

William Herbert, 3rd Earl of Pembroke. *Right* Philip, 4th Earl of Pembroke, and 1st Earl of Montgomery.

tion of the First Folio to the 'incomparable brethren' may have been ambiguous. 'You could look at it from a good point of view that they were both considered to be two of the most outstanding people in the land; or you could look at it the other way, which is that one was very good where the other was very bad, and therefore they couldn't be compared to each other.'

Philip, made Earl of Montgomery by James I, was hot-blooded and boorish, and was as unpopular at Court as his elder brother was popular. But they both held positions of great influence. James commended Philip particularly to his heir, and at Charles I's Coronation Pembroke carried the crown and Montgomery the spurs. After King Charles' first visit to Wilton he was so enchanted with it that he returned regularly. In the words of John Aubrey, 'King Charles the first did love Wilton above all places, and came thither every summer. It was he that did put Philip, Earl of Pembroke, upon making this magnificent garden and grotto, and to new build that side of the house that fronts the garden.'

The King urged the skills of Inigo Jones to Pembroke, but the great architect was too busy on the Queen's House at Greenwich, so Isaac de Caus began the work in 1633. He laid out a vast formal garden extending 1,000 feet southwards across the river, and 400 feet wide, with parterres, arbours, walkways, fountains, pools, and a great grotto with trick water effects that alone cost £2,000. De Caus' plans for an enormous south front were curtailed for lack of money, and the splendid facade we see today is only about half the length of the original plan. (Once again over-ambitious and monstrously grandiose building plans were fortunately prevented by lack of funds.)

Philip, who had succeeded his brother as the 4th Earl in 1630, habitually thought on the grand scale. He commissioned the huge family portrait by Van Dyck that occupies the whole of one wall in the Double Cube Room, but it was a few years before it could be brought to Wilton. Between its painting and its hanging here came first the Civil War and then the great fire at Wilton.

Philip's choleric temper and occasional physical assaults on people did not endear him to to his precise and unbending monarch, who was so enraged when he voted for Strafford's impeachment that he dismissed him from the office of Lord Chamberlain. Pembroke became allied with the Parliamentary opposition and joined several delegations to the King which unsuccessfully tried to bend him to Parliament's will. The King found it particularly hard to bear the opposition of the master of Wilton who in his eyes had become a turncoat. At the same time many of Pembroke's allies believed he was only concerned to retain the ownership of his estates, and suspected him of secretly giving money to the King although the House of Lords acquitted him of that charge. His sympathies seem to have fluctuated right to the end. He spoke in the House of Lords against the proposal to set up a special Court to try the King, later attended the execution and watched the King step on to the scaffold, but left the scene before the axe fell.

To many of Pembroke's Royalist enemies it must have been a singularly tasteless coincidence that it was the year of the King's death, 1649, that Philip embarked on the famous rebuilding of Wilton after the fire, under the eye of Charles I's favourite architect, Inigo Jones. Jones was now 77, so he left most of the detailed work to his nephew John Webb. Neither Jones nor Pembroke

The garden to the west of the House.

Van Dyck's largest family group (17 ft by 11 ft), of the 4th Earl and his family. The 'angels' are three children who died in infancy.

lived to see the completion of the seven great state rooms behind the south front, which include two of the most famous apartments in the country, the Single Cube and the Double Cube. The first is 30 feet by 30 feet by 30 feet, and the second is exactly twice as long. The white painted pine panelling is richly decorated with carvings of fruit, flowers, figures, scrollwork and the family monogram all picked out in gold leaf. The painted ceilings in both rooms are of allegorical scenes. In the Single Cube it is 'Daedalus and Icarus' by Giuseppe Cesari, and in the Double Cube Thomas de Critz painted the story of Perseus.

In the Double Cube all the pictures except one are by Van Dyck, including the vast family portrait, eventually transported to Wilton as three rolled pieces of canvas – as the present Earl of Pembroke says, 'It's quite a hairy thought of it being trundled down on the very rough roads.' Looking at the portraits of King Charles, his Queen, and their three children in this splendid setting it is hard to remember that the 4th Earl, whose likeness shares their company, took the Parliamentary side.

When Charles II returned to the throne, he too visited the house so loved by his father. He would have seen another family likeness in one of the portraits in the Single Cube. Henriette de Kerouaille, wife of the 7th Lord Pembroke, was the sister of Louise de Kerouaille (one of Charles II's favourite mistresses, from whom the Dukes of Richmond are descended). It was

Henriette de Kerouaille, wife of Philip, 7th Earl of Pembroke.

probably a stormy marriage since the 7th Earl was not one of the present Earl's most admired ancestors. 'He was known as the most violent homicide of his age. He is reputed to have killed something like 26 people, which I think is probably an exaggeration, but undoubtedly he was a very unsavoury, disreputable character, a drunk who got into constant brawling.

He was rather inclined when provoked just simply to draw his sword and stick it into the nearest person.' Tried on a murder charge in 1678 he was lucky to be convicted only of manslaughter. As a peer he was let off with a warning, but after several other duels and brawls in which men died he was confined to Wilton, where he died of drink at the early age of 30, to the great relief of the world at large, but leaving no will, and debts of £20,000.

The Double Cube has been used for receptions, banquets, balls and concerts, but its most important event took place during the Second World War when it was the operations room of Southern Command, and the D-Day landings were planned here. At that time the pictures were covered over, but today the room looks as it did when it was first completed in 1653, though most of the furniture is of a later date, by Chippendale and William Kent.

Another of the Inigo Jones rooms is the Colonnade Room, which used to be the State Bedroom. It has a beautifully decorated ceiling, dating from about a hundred years later than the room itself, by the French painter Andien de Clermont. Of course it may have been partially obscured from view by the four-poster bed which almost certainly occupied the room at the time, but which, much to the present Earl of Pembroke's regret, has long disappeared from the house, along with all the others. 'I don't know what's happened to them, it's very sad. I love four-poster beds, but there's not a single one left in the whole house.'

The Colonnade Room also features a seventeenth century painting of the Madonna surrounded by a garland of flowers, by Giovanni Battista Salvi and Mario Nuzzi. It is, as the Earl of Pembroke says, 'very pretty, but there's no great significance to it'. However it is probably one of the most popular paintings in the house with visitors: 'I think we sell more postcards of that than anything else.'

We think of Inigo Jones as the great English architect, but the classical Italian and French influences on him can be clearly seen above the mantel-pieces and doorways at Wilton. Passing through into the Great Ante Room brings you to the man himself, in the form of a small statue by Rysbrach standing on top of the fireplace. His eye seems to be looking disapprovingly at where his great painted staircase once stood, before it was ripped out in the nineteenth century to make room for Wyatt's cloisters. The present Earl feels it was rather a sacrilege to pull down a large part of an Inigo Jones house: 'You wouldn't be allowed to do that today in a hurry would you?'

Opposite the statuette is the Earl's favourite picture, of Rembrandt's mother, and he is angered by art experts who suggest that it might not be a genuine Rembrandt. 'There's an awful lot of hypocrisy goes on I think in the art world. This painting, which has been admired by so many people for so many years, now because people say it's not Rembrandt they tend to disregard it, although of course it's exactly the same painting today as it's always been.'

The 7th Earl was succeeded by his brother Thomas, who restored the family name and its fortunes. When he drew his sword it was in a worthier cause than any of his murderous brothers. Once he defended Nell Gwyn's

Rembrandt's Mother, painted c.1629.

honour at the Duke's Theatre when her performance was greeted with a shout of 'whore', and again on a much greater affair of State when as Lord Lieutenant of Wiltshire he commanded the local militia against Monmouth's rebellion. Characteristically the obtuse James II made an enemy of Pembroke, and he was one of the peers who invited William of Orange 'to come to take the government of the nation into his hands'.

It was Thomas who gathered at Wilton the great collection of pictures, the many valuable books, and the large number of sculptures that are now displayed in the upper cloisters, including the Arundel marbles and Mazarin busts. It was he too who imported the French weavers and founded the Wilton Royal Carpet Factory, which has made the name synonymous with quality in house-furnishing anywhere. He instilled the same enthusiasm for the arts in his son, Henry Herbert, but Henry's greatest love was architecture, and he came to be known as the 'Architect Earl'.

His claim to this sobriquet was endorsed in a most uncharacteristically generous way by the normally waspish Horace Walpole: 'The soul of Inigo Jones, who had been patronised by his ancestors, seemed still to hover over its favourite, Wilton, and to have assisted the muses of arts in the education of this noble person. The towers, the chambers, the scenes which Holbein, Jones and Van Dyck had decorated, and which Earl Thomas had enriched with the spoils of the best ages, received the last touches of beauty from Earl Henry's hand.'

Henry and his Clerk of Works, Roger Morris, designed houses for George II in Richmond Park and Lady Suffolk in Twickenham, a water tower at Houghton, and the memorial column at Blenheim, though Pembroke soon joined the list of the Duchess of Marlborough's other architects in falling foul of her vicious and complaining tongue. But his name is most associated with the two famous bridges – old Westminster Bridge, and the Palladian Bridge over the little River Nadder at Wilton. (The latter was so much admired that it was almost exactly copied by Kent at Stowe, and by Wood at Prior Park, near Bath.)

To give the bridge its proper setting the Earl cleared away de Caus' huge formal garden, waterworks and all, replacing it with the sweeping lawns dotted with cedars that are now admired in their full maturity. The river was widened and brought nearer the house, and the bridge was so positioned that both it and the house are seen to best advantage from each other. Five arches and a balustrade join the two temple-porticoes at each end, and a gentle waterfall ripples underneath it. It took three years to build and is one of the great glories of Wilton. An inspiration to artists and photographers alike, the version painted by Sir Winston Churchill now stands in the Tudor entrance.

The Architect Earl was 57 when he died, and his only son Henry came into his inheritance at the age of sixteen. He completed his education with a

Grand Tour of Europe that lasted four years, and in 1756 married the second daughter of the Duke of Marlborough. Soon afterwards he was appointed Lord Lieutenant of Wiltshire, and two years later became ADC to George II. He had a successful military career, attaining the rank of Major-General. A great horseman, in 1762 he published *Military Equitation or a Method of Breaking Horses and Teaching Soldiers to Ride*, which remained the standard work for the British Army for years. This drew on the methods of the continental riding-schools, and he commissioned an extraordinary set of 55 gouache paintings of the Spanish Riding School in Vienna, which now hang in the large Smoking Room at Wilton. They look rather comic and unnatural, but their accuracy is vouched for by the fact that they were done by Baron D'Eisenberg, riding master to the Emperor Francis I of Austria. The present Earl shares his ancestor's interest in riding, even though his busy schedule as TV director and the demands of running Wilton itself prevent him from doing as much as he would like. 'In some respects I'm rather a frustrated jockey. I'd love to have been a jockey, but I'm not quite the right

The gouaches of the Spanish Riding School, painted for the 10th Earl by the Austrian Emperor's riding master, Baron D'Eisenberg, in 1755.

size.' (An understatement, coming from a man who stands well over six feet!)

The 10th Earl continued the building work at Wilton, commissioning Sir William Chambers to design the Triumphal Arch over the north entrance, crowned by the equestrian statue of Marcus Aurelius, which is the first thing the visitor sees today. To his contemporaries he seemed to have the golden touch, and fortune smiled on all his activities. But then suddenly he threw everything up to elope with a Miss Kitty Hunter. After she had borne his child she transferred her affections to his friend Lord Bristol, who fathered her second child. Henry was reconciled with his wife, in spite of other infidelities, but eventually she left him for good. This produced one happy and unique artistic result. In the Colonnade Room there are two nearly identical portraits by Joshua Reynolds of Lady Pembroke and her son George, because she had to leave the first one behind when she left Wilton and asked the painter for another copy. In the second one the only difference is that she is wearing a veil, and now they can be closely compared.

George was as close to his mother in life as he is in both these double portraits and it is hardly surprising that he was unwilling to take much notice of his father, who was brimming over with parental advice and exhortation.

(A & B) The 11th Earl as a boy with his mother, Lady Elizabeth Spencer. Both portraits were painted by Sir Joshua Reynolds, and now hang for comparison in the Colonnade Room.

George spent five years on his Grand Tour, and was inundated with letters telling him how to spend his time most usefully. But Henry's appeals to his son to marry an heiress fell on deaf ears. George chose as his bride a penniless cousin, Elizabeth Beauclerk, and was probably not surprised to receive a remonstration from Lord Pembroke, 'You know how very much the situation of our affairs stand in need of at least thirty thousand pounds. I now fear them irretrievable for our time, at least; it would have been lucky for us, had you found a thirty thousand pounder as agreeable to you as Elizabeth.'

But it was the father who proved the feckless one, neglecting his estates by his frequent travels abroad, and it was George, the 11th Earl, who undertook the next great period of improvement and change at Wilton. In accordance with family practice he chose the principal architect of the day, James Wyatt, who had succeeded Sir William Chambers as Surveyor-General and Controller of the Works. But the public duties of this post had now so increased that Wyatt had less time to spare for his private clients, and Wilton not only lacked a Clerk of Works of the calibre of Roger Morris, it seems not to have had one at all at this time.

In the first year of the nineteenth century when George received Wyatt's plans he was also offered a Marquessate by William Pitt. He consulted a cousin, Lord Carnarvon, on both matters. Carnarvon advised him to decline the latter, but approved the former with one reservation. He thought that Wyatt's design would give a large house the convenience and comfort of a small one, but he feared 'that you who do not feel the great difference between a Marquis and a Earl, will not feel the wide distinction between a Cloysters and a passage, and be satisfied with too little Gothick ornament in that part'.

Wyatt's most advantageous feature was the double-storeyed cloister around all four sides of the internal courtyard, which allowed access to any room directly without having to go all the way round from room to room. It is light and airy, and in addition to the various sculptures it holds interesting paintings and collections of medals. Wyatt built a library on the west front, although most of the contents have been dispersed since the First World War, and a Gothic hall inside the Tudor tower on the east front, but he has been most criticised for his changes to the north front, which became the main entrance, as it still is today. For some reason he raised the level of the forecourt by ten feet, which made the entrance hall at ground level, when such a great house really needs a flight of steps to give it an appropriately grand entrance.

Changing it from east to north necessitated diverting the old road from Salisbury, which brought several water-meadows into the private grounds of Wilton. While he was doing all this, at the considerable expense of £200,000, Lord Pembroke also much improved his estates and his income from them, thus finally discrediting his father's predictions of doom if he married for love. After Elizabeth died in 1793 he remained a widower for fifteen years before again choosing a beautiful wife, Catherine Woronzow, daughter of the former Russian Ambassador in London. Count Woronzow's bemedalled portrait hangs in the Colonnade Room, between the pair of his son-in-law as a small boy by Reynolds.

The Cloisters by James Wyatt.

George had a son by each marriage, and they turned out to have very different temperaments. Robert, the elder son, rushed into an unwise marriage in Sicily, which did not last, and lived out most of his days abroad with a mistress and large family. His half-brother, Sidney Herbert, was clever and industrious, becoming an M.P. and Secretary of War. By arrangement with Robert he lived in and maintained Wilton. He is most famous for sending Florence Nightingale to the Crimean War, and then chairing the Royal Commission set up to inquire into the sanitary conditions of the Army, but his efforts in support of her work did not bring him much peace. Lady Palmerston complained to her husband about him being 'half-Russian', and the Lady with the Lamp herself was not an easy ally. The present Earl has read their correspondence at Wilton: 'We have a lot of letters here, I think it was a platonic relationship but they were very close friends. She was a very tough, demanding woman, and I think in the end the strain of being War Minister, and the strain put on by her probably killed him. He died in his early fifties, but he was always to me a very romantic figure.'

Sidney died at Wilton in 1861 worn out by his public exertions, and the 12th Earl ended his dissolute life in Paris the following year. It is an instructive contrast. The black sheep in other noble families have often brought ruin to their families and estates, but the Pembroke line always seems to have had the strength to bounce back from the two or three Earls whose activities could have lost Wilton to their heirs. Today the house has a solidity and serenity that looks permanent and secure. The present Earl believes this is in part because the unbroken line of Herberts has managed over the past 450 years not only to hold on to Wilton 'by a combination of good luck and good judgment', but also, bar one or two exceptions, to have improved it gradually over a very long period. 'Most of my ancestors have contributed something to the house.' Wandering through from one beautiful room to the next, with its decorations, pictures and furniture from the last five centuries, one is constantly reminded of the unbroken family line by the repetition of the monogram HPM (for Herbert, Pembroke and Montgomery), underlined by the family motto 'Ung je serveray', the old French spelling translated as 'One I will serve'.

The present Earl of Pembroke believes this too can be interpreted in more than one way. 'My father always believed it was God, but I think earlier ancestors believed it was the Sovereign.' He is naturally keen to hand on Wilton to his son, and takes the responsibilities of his own tenure seriously. 'I think I would be slightly untruthful to say that I never felt it was something of a burden, because it obviously is. But you then have to hit yourself quite hard and say how dare you think of it as a burden, it's the most beautiful place on earth. Stop complaining and get on with it.' Getting on with it means keeping it in good repair, opening it to the public for tours and events to pay for its upkeep, and always bearing in mind how many of the great houses have been lost in this century. 'You can destroy them very quickly, but if you do destroy them, you're destroying a heritage.'

The family monogram of Herbert, Pembroke and Montgomery.

UPPARK

WHEN Humphry Repton was preparing his plans for improvements at Uppark in the early nineteenth century he was so enraptured by its existing charms that he asked, 'What rarity can retain its rareness at Uppark where all that is good is common – and all that is common is more than commonly good?' His aim was to preserve its essential character, and what is so remarkable about Uppark is the way in which this character has remained preserved unchanged right through the Victorian period and our own. It has been called a 'Sleeping Beauty house' and entering it the visitor steps straight back into a perfect representation of what an eighteenth century predecessor would have seen. It is thought that H. G. Wells may have got his idea of the Time Machine from his childhood at Uppark, where his mother was housekeeper to the old ladies who refused to change anything in it.

Today Uppark is in the hands of the National Trust, which has maintained the house as it was. Uppark has only had six generations of owners who have lived in it as their home, and perhaps their extraordinary longevity is due to the bracing air of its elevated position. As its name implies it is built in parkland at the top of a hill, above the village of South Harting in West Sussex, not far from Goodwood. The Duke of Wellington considered buying it before he chose Stratfield Saye, but he took one look at the steep hill leading to Uppark on the crest of the South Downs and changed his mind, because it would have cost him new horses every eighteen months.

The approach up through the woods to the north entrance does not prepare you for the spectacular view to the south, as the rolling parkland falls away to Hayling Island and the sea, and the Isle of Wight can be seen on the horizon. Looking back at the south front from a distance the rectangular red-brick house set off with stone and white paintwork looks rather like a large doll's house just set down on the hill (an impression reinforced by the sight of the similar-shaped large eighteenth century doll's house to be found inside).

No house could have been built in this position until the late seventeenth century, since until then there was no known way of pumping water so far uphill. The solution was found by a member of the Ford family, which owned the Manor of Harting and Uppark. Sir Edward Ford had fought on

149

the King's side in the Civil War, but his claim to fame rests with Cromwell who employed him to improve London's water-supply. Anthony à Wood recorded in his *Athenae Oxoniensis*, 'Edward Ford of Uppark was a most ingenious mechanist and being encouraged by Oliver and invited by the citizens of London in 1656, he raised the Thames water into all the highest streets of the city, ninety-three feet high in four eight-inch pipes, to the wonder of all men, and the Honour of the Nation, with a rare engine of his own invention, done at his own charge and in one year's time.' A development of his 'rare engine' carried water from South Harting 350 feet up to the house his grandson built at Uppark around 1690.

Ford, who was Lord Grey of Werke and later the Earl of Tankerville, had a weakness for intrigue that could have cost him his life. His impetuosity soon revealed itself, when he ran away with his wife's sister, Henrietta Berkeley, but then and later he escaped the consequences of his actions. Lord Berkeley was outraged by the man who had ruined the lives of two of his daughters and took him to court, but failed to have him punished. Grey was a close friend of the Duke of Monmouth, and was said by some to be the latter's evil genius. When they were both discovered to be mixed up in the Rye House Plot to kill Charles II and the Duke of York, Monmouth fled but Grey was arrested and committed to the Tower.

Unlike Algernon Sidney of Penshurst, another of the conspirators who lost his head this time, Grey escaped to join Monmouth abroad, and landed in England with him to try and seize the Crown when Charles II died in 1685. Grey was an incompetent commander of the cavalry at Sedgemoor, and was captured after that crushing defeat. He evaded joining Monmouth on the block by turning King's evidence and implicating his friends, getting off with a heavy fine. He proclaimed his undying loyalty to James II: 'My own inclination will ever oblige me to sacrifice the life you give to your service when you please to command it.' But when his King did command it, against William of Orange's invasion in 1688, Grey pleaded incapacity by gout, and was rewarded by the new King with a Privy Councillorship and the Earldom of Tankerville. At last secure in royal favour he embarked on the building of Uppark. His architect is thought to have been William Talman, Controller of the King's Works to William III, which may explain its echoes of the Dutch style – 'a sort of Amsterdam town house standing nakedly in this wonderful landscape' is how the National Trust Administrator, John Eyre, describes it. The main entrance was to the east, which must have made a more impressive scenic approach than the present one to the north. In nearly every other respect the exterior of the house is still as it was originally built.

The passing of Uppark from the Tankervilles to the Fetherstonhaughs came about through a slightly curious bequest. The first Sir Henry Fetherstonhaugh was born in the same year as the first Lord Tankerville, but lived

151

nearly twice as long, to the age of 92. As neither he nor his nine brothers and sisters had any children, he left his great fortune – he was one of the first northern 'coal capitalists' – to a young namesake, Matthew Fetherstonhaugh, in the hope that he could thus revive the baronetcy and settle in the south. Matthew must have graphically described the rigours of his Northumberland childhood to his son, for Harry wrote much later that his ancestors 'knew no more of luxurious agreements than the Laplanders, and I might have been shivering in the old Gothic hall at Fetherstone Castle with only a frigid sense of its antiquity'.

So in 1746 Matthew gained his baronetcy, and in the same year he bought Uppark from the third Lord Tankerville for £19,000 and immediately began acquiring the surrounding property. He showed good judgment in all he touched, including his choice of wife, Sarah Lethieullier, a woman of fortune and good taste to match her husband's. She brought with her to Uppark the doll's house made in the 1720s, the time of her own childhood, though even then it is doubtful if children were allowed to play with it, and now it is much too valuable to risk damaging. The contents are all genuine period pieces, the miniature silver is hallmarked, of great value and of very high quality, and the tiny footmen are wearing the livery of that period, correct down to the last detail. There are nine rooms, so that even in miniature the whole thing stands more than 7 feet high, 7 feet long and 3 feet deep.

The Lethieullier coat of arms sits in the pediment of the doll's house, and Sarah and her husband replaced the Tankerville arms in the pediment of Uppark with their own, when they set about transforming the interiors of Uppark in what elsewhere would have been only the first of many redecorations, but here was almost the last. They did little to the Staircase Hall, which today contains a large picture by Tillemans of the house as it was, before they pulled down the stables and other outbuildings to the east to improve the view. Portraits of Matthew and Sarah hang near the door as if to greet the visitors to their home.

Their main alterations were to the staterooms of the house, replacing much of the late seventeenth century painted panelling with flock wallpapers, creating delicately moulded plaster ceilings, and raising the level of the original first floor. They went off on their Grand Tour of Europe from 1749 to 1751, and brought back many of the works of art we still see today. In the eighteenth century, paintings were often bought or commissioned to order as souvenirs by well-to-do travellers, as John Eyre explains. 'Where we would have bought picture postcards they just had oil paintings knocked up for them at the appropriate time.' This is not to say that all were necessarily of poor quality. Canaletto in Venice and Ruys in Naples produced many fine paintings for this purpose, and among those chosen by Matthew and Sarah is a rare set of four pictures of Naples. Some of the pictures they bought

152

specifically to hang in certain rooms, but in other cases the room was modelled around them. Several pictures in the Saloon are built into the walls, and their son later commissioned Repton to design the built-in bookcases, which he decorated in the same style as the rest of the room.

The Saloon gives the effect of a double cube room reminiscent of the one at Wilton in its proportions. Built a century later than the creation of Inigo Jones and Webb, it is smaller, much lighter in style, and the ivory-coloured walls and ceiling are decorated with intricate and delicate traceries of gold leaf. The ceiling was raised about four and a half feet to achieve the right proportions, which had the same effect upstairs as the similar operation in

The 18th Century Doll's House.

the Ballroom at Goodwood House, foreshortening the height of the bed-rooms and raising their floor-levels well above the bottom of the windows. Sir Matthew was a friend of the 4th Duke of Richmond and they frequently visited each other's homes, so it is not surprising that they both did the same thing to the grandest room in each of their houses. Sir Matthew took an active part in country affairs as a magistrate, where he cracked down heavily on smuggling, but although he became an M.P. he cut no figure in national politics. He made a greater mark as a Fellow of the Royal Society, and frequently conducted experiments with electricity in the Red Drawing Room at Uppark, to the entertainment, instruction and often alarm of his guests.

Sir Matthew and Sarah Fetherstonhaugh.

Sir Matthew died in 1774 at the age of 60 (a mere youngster by usual Fetherstonhaugh standards), leaving his estate to his only son Harry, an impressionable and impulsive youth of 20. His mother tried to keep her hand on the family accounts, but found this increasingly difficult. The historian Edward Gibbon knew the family well and after one visit in 1775 he wrote, 'Sir Harry is very civil and good humoured. But from the unavoidable temper of youth, I fear he will cost many a tear to Lady F. She consults everybody, but has neither authority nor plan.'

Harry was at Oxford when his father died, and he went on his Grand Tour shortly afterwards. He had his portrait painted in Rome by Batoni

The Saloon, where Sir Harry Fetherstonhaugh married his dairymaid, Mary Ann Bullock.

against a classical background, in the painter's characteristic style for visiting Englishmen, and it hangs in the Red Drawing Room, showing a tall slim figure with a long nose and sandy hair. He does not look a particularly romantic or even sexually attractive figure, but his looks belie his nature (his own mother once referred to him as 'the Prodigal Son'), because his adult life began and ended with two passionate and rather astonishing romances.

He was one of the earliest lovers of Emma Hart, later Lady Hamilton and Nelson's great love. She was only fifteen when Harry met her, a blacksmith's daughter whose stunning beauty had landed her a job as a model in a kind of nightclub, the 'Temple of Aesculapius' in the Adelphi. He took her under his wing and installed her on the estate at Uppark. When Lady Fetherstonhaugh was away Emma is reputed to have entertained Sir Harry and his friends by dancing on the dining-table 'in a state of nature'. John Eyre doubts that this phrase meant that she danced actually in the nude: 'It's all a question of knickers. They weren't invented you see, so that in those days when a lady danced on the table all sorts of exciting things happened.'

One of Harry's friends that Emma met at Uppark was the diarist Charles Greville who was to play a major role in her life, which see-sawed from poverty to wealthy protection and back to near-destitution. After a year at Uppark she was packed off to Cheshire, six months' pregnant and with virtually no money, while Harry was away hunting at Leicester. She wrote in desperation to Greville, in her always individual spelling.

'Yesterday did I receive your kind letter. It put me in some spirits, for believe me, I am allmost distracktid. I have never heard from Sir H. and he is not at Lechster now. I am sure. What shall I dow? Good God. What shall I dow? I have wrote 7 letters, and no anser. I can't come to town for want of money. I have not a farthing to bless my self with, and I think my friends looks cooly on me. I think so. O.G. what shall I dow? what shall I dow? O how your letter affected me. wen you wished me happiness. O.G. that I was in your possession or was in Sir H. What a happy girl would I have been! "Girl indeed". what else am I but a girl in distress – in reall distress. For God's sake, G, write the minet you get this, and only tell me what I am to dow.'

Reading that heartfelt appeal today one cannot fail to be stirred to sympathy, and it is to Greville's credit that he answered it by taking her into his house at Paddington with her mother. (The baby is more likely to have been his than Harry's.) When he tired of her after some years he assured her future by despatching her to his rich widowed uncle, Sir William Hamilton, British Ambassador in Naples, who took her as a reluctant mistress, but five years later married her. As Lady Hamilton she stepped on to the national stage through her famous love-affair with Nelson.

After Nelson's death at Trafalgar in 1805 Emma was soon in financial difficulties, and turned again to her first protector, begging him for a loan of £500. Harry responded immediately, and her IOU still remains with her letters to him since he never presented it to Coutts Bank, an act of greater generosity since she never was in a position to honour it. He seems to have paid off some of her later debts as well.

Throughout the years between his first and last contacts with Emma Sir Harry had remained a bachelor, and lived his life according to that state and to his social position. He became an M.P. like his father but played as little part in Parliament, and soon became disillusioned with its intrigues. His preferred pastimes were hunting and racing, the basis for his close friendship with the Prince of Wales, later Regent, later still George IV. 'Prinny' made frequent visits here from Brighton and matched his horses in races against Sir Harry's. Two racing cups in the dining-room date from that period, one elegant and simple in Georgian classical style, the other 'Brighton vulgar', bearing the Prince of Wales's feathers and known as the Uppark Cup.

Entertaining the Prince and his retinue so often was a considerable expense. Sir Harry's mother kept precise accounts of the necessary provisioning for three days in 1784: '2 Bucks, a Welsh sheep, a doz. Ducks, – 4 Hams, dozens of pigeons, and Rabbits, Flitches of Bacon, Lobsters and Prawns; a Turtle of 120 lbs.; 166 lbs. of Butter; 376 Eggs, 67 Chickens; 23 Pints of Cream, 30 lbs. of Coffee, 10 lbs. of Fine Tea; and three lbs. of common tea.' This proved not to have been enough, since more 'Bucks' and sheep were added later. Harry had a famous chef, Moget, whose feats on the great roasting-spit in the kitchen were not the least of the attractions of Uppark for the Prince, though he also rhapsodised about 'the most beautiful Spot of Ground I believe that England can produce'.

He even had his own room there, and wrote in terms that indicate how frequent his visits were.

'Dear Sir Harry,
I hope you will not think me very troublesome if I beg of you to give me my old Bed at Up Park on Sunday night. I shall endeavour to be with you by dinner between five and six o'clock. Nobody but General Hulse will come with me. I am
very sincerely Yours
George P.

Brighton;
August 14th 1795'

(Today the red damask coverings on the Prince's 'old Bed' have been restored to their original condition).

But few people stayed friends with the Prince Regent forever, and his dear

157

friend Sir Harry was no exception. For 25 years they were close companions in sporting, eating and drinking, and then they appear to have quarrelled, though the cause is still a mystery. By 1811 the rift seems to have become irreparable between them. Sir Harry felt the estrangement keenly, especially when he was denied an invitation to a great fête at Carlton House. 'All London will be there, and be dressed magnificently; and of course WE shall not be of it.'

He consoled himself with sport at Uppark, where the noise of shooting parties can have hardly ceased. The Duke of Argyll wrote gleefully, 'Famous sport at Uppark, 408 pheasants in 4 days, and 835 things.' But these diversions were beginning to pall on Harry, 'I really can amuse myself very well without that incessant discharge of field-pieces so essential to all fashionable sportsmen of the present generation.' His thoughts began to turn to less destructive pastimes, and to making his own mark on his home. He had always retained his interest in the arts, and took advantage of the brief break in the Napoleonic Wars during the Peace of Amiens in 1802 to pay a quick visit to France, and buy some furniture (much of which went down in the *Titanic* in 1912, on its way to the Metropolitan Museum of Art in New York). He turned to Humphry Repton, the great landscape gardener, for advice on the house as well as the gardens. The two men were much the same age, and Repton was also aggrieved with the Prince Regent for rejecting his plans for the Brighton Pavilion and passing him over as Surveyor-General, so they had much in common. What began as a professional relationship developed into a close personal friendship until Repton's death.

Repton prepared his plans in his usual way, compiling one of his famous 'Red Books' with watercolours, showing the place both before and after his improvements. The two men decided to build a new north entrance, with a pillared portico and a long corridor to the main part of the house, reminiscent on a smaller scale of the porticoed East Front and corridor to the Sculpture Hall at Broadlands, which may have inspired Repton's designs.

Repton's biggest transformation inside was the Dining Room where he put in a new chimney piece, and mirrors in the four corners of the room set at such an angle that there are multiple reflections. The most inspired touch was the circular stained glass window put in the north window of the Serving Room, lit by oil lamps and candles from behind at night, so that the colours flooded into the Dining Room when the double doors were thrown open to admit the food. As a result the ambience of this room is now considerably changed from the one in which Emma Hart kicked up her heels for the young Sir Harry.

One of the most unusual features of the domestic arrangements is the system of underground passages built by Sir Harry and Humphry Repton to connect the kitchens with the basement of the house. Food was brought over

The 'American' tapestry, showing the loss of the American Colonies.

on wooden trolleys and kept warm by charcoal heaters, carried up to the Serving Room behind the Dining Room and put on hot plates until served. This system lasted for nearly a century, and during that time the servants would have enjoyed hotter food than their masters. It seems a high price to pay for keeping the smells of the kitchen away from the living rooms in the main house, but even so the Fetherstonhaughs were better off than the nobility in much grander houses, who can hardly ever have eaten a hot meal in their lives.

By now Sir Harry was over 60 and still unmarried. The ending of the Napoleonic Wars opened up Europe to English visitors again and Harry was briefly tempted by the idea of selling Uppark to the Duke of Wellington for

The Dining Room, by Humphry Repton.

his country seat. He wrote to the Duchess of Richmond, 'I really see nothing for it unless I make over Uppark to the Duke and retire to a warm climate, as every old batchelor should at my time of life.' But Duke and Baronet both changed their minds about the sale, and Sir Harry's desire to live abroad was assuaged by two long visits to France in 1819 and 1824. By then he was approaching 70 and getting increasingly lonely, but was about to find companionship and comfort in his old age in a marriage that astounded his contemporaries, has come down to us as one of the great romances, and did more than anything to preserve Uppark as a time-capsule.

One day walking on the lawn near the pretty pillared dairy to the west of the house he heard a young girl singing, and on enquiring learnt that she was the dairymaid, Mary Ann Bullock. His walks near the dairy became more frequent and one day he went in and proposed marriage to Mary Ann. He did not stay for an immediate answer, but told her that if she would have him, she was to cut a slice out of the leg of mutton that was coming up for dinner. When it arrived the slice was cut.

They were married in the Saloon at Uppark on September 12th, 1825, where a copy of the marriage certificate can now be seen. It is clear that 'Ann' is the only element of Mary Ann's signature that she actually wrote herself, but even this was a significant improvement on most of her contemporaries from the village, who could only manage 'X' – his or her mark. He was 71, Mary Ann was 20. The age-gap was as great as the class-barrier, but they lived happily together as man and wife for another 21 years. He sent her off to Paris to educate her, brought her young sister Frances into the household and engaged a governess to teach her, and later he and his wife established the school in Harting village. But educational improvement did not impress Society, which was far more baffled by his marriage than it had been by his youthful liaison with Emma Hart, and both his friends and hers found it difficult to understand their match. Many local people believed she 'led him up the garden path', although it seems that Sir Harry may have wanted to be led. As John Eyre says, he was probably like many old bachelors in country houses who dreamed of producing an heir. Even though this never happened, Mary Ann made the old Baronet happier in the last two decades of his life than he had been in any of the previous seven, and looked after his physical comfort with tender understanding as his powers began to fade.

He died in the Prince Regent's favourite bed in 1846, aged 92, leaving everything to his wife. She outlived him by nearly 30 years and during that time refused to change anything at Uppark, keeping it exactly as Harry always had. Intelligent and thrifty, she ruled the estate with a firm hand, and was not overawed by her astonishing leap up the social scale. 'It is a very good thing to be a Downstairs person as well as an Upstairs person,' she said when she was obliged to dismiss the head Gamekeeper for drunkenness, without affecting the day's activities. She proudly described herself in the census of 1851 as 'a farmer of 5,146 acres, employing 203 labourers', to whom she could be generous and helpful if they behaved themselves, and she took an active interest in the welfare of the local community.

She died in 1874 leaving Uppark to her sister Frances, who assumed the name of Fetherstonhaugh and lived on there with her former governess Ann Sutherland for another 20 years. They too only wanted to ' 'ave everything as Sir 'Arry 'ad it', and so Uppark was preserved untouched by the Victorian 'modernisations' that have left their mark elsewhere.

That time has been preserved in another way, through the pen of H. G. Wells, whose mother became housekeeper here in 1880. His memories of

The Dairy.

162

Mary Ann as an old lady.

Uppark as a small boy are recorded in his *Experiment in Autobiography*: 'The place had a great effect on me; it retained a vitality that altogether over-shadowed the ebbing tide of upstairs life, the two elderly ladies in the parlour following their shrunken routines.' Wells had further reason to be grateful for the old ladies' 'shrunken routines', however, since it gave him ample opportunity to get into the library, hiding between the double doors until the coast was clear, before 'nipping through to feast himself on Tom Paine and Montesquieu and Voltaire and all the treasures within'. Although the great days had gone by the time Wells arrived with his mother he had the imagination to see that houses like Uppark stood for something rather special:

'Out of such houses came the Royal Society . . . the first museums and laboratories and picture galleries, gentle manners, good writing and nearly all that is worth while in our civilisation today. Their culture, like the culture of the ancient world, rested on a toiling class. Nobody bothered very much about that, but it has been far more through the curiosity of and enterprise and free deliberate thinking of these independent gentlemen than through any other influences, that modern machinery and economic organisation have developed so as to abolish at last the harsh necessity for any toiling class whatever.'

At Uppark today it is possible to see the conditions in which 'the toiling classes' worked and lived below stairs, as they have been preserved in the same way as the splendour upstairs. The dairy where the great romance began still stands, and the view from the seat outside it is the best final glimpse of the house, glowing gently in the westering sun.

The Kitchen in the basement.

SUTTON PLACE

EVERY other house in this book has sought to preserve the spirit and character of the past as much as possible, but Sutton Place is the great exception. The outside appearance is of a well-preserved and attractive Tudor house, but inside it is an Aladdin's cave of art and artefacts from many ages, while the gardens have been created only in this decade by the doyen of English landscape architects. This extraordinary transformation has been carried out at a cost of millions, from the fortune of an American billionaire recluse, Stanley Seeger, who has created a Trust in his name to run Sutton Place as a cultural centre with regular exhibitions, lectures and concerts. Parties of visitors are taken on guided tours of the house and gardens in small groups, but only by advance appointment.

This juxtaposition of old and new has aroused controversy in the world of the arts, and been the subject of a Department of Environment public inquiry, but the great interest for the visitor to Sutton Place is to see what happens to a historic house in the 1980s, when money is no object and the decision has been taken to convert it to a very different use from that of its previous owners.

There is a legend of an ancient curse laid on the place in the eleventh century by Edith, the spurned Queen of the misogynist Edward the Confessor, and certainly the dark side of life has been no stranger to Sutton Place. Indeed both the date and the reason why Henry VIII gave the estate to Sir Richard Weston in 1521 are shadowed with violence. Weston was one of the Duke of Buckingham's judges at his trial for treason, and he received his reward of Sutton Place from the King on the very day Buckingham's head was severed from his body.

Sir Richard was one of the great survivors in a period when that achievement required some skill. He had been one of Henry VII's trusted advisers and was one of the 'sad and ancient knights' who brought a touch of *gravitas* to the more flamboyant court of Henry VIII. He accompanied the King to the Field of the Cloth of Gold, he became Wolsey's man but survived the Cardinal's fall, and in 1536 he survived a much more perilous association. His son Francis was a close friend of Anne Boleyn, was accused of adultery with the Queen, and was beheaded like her. But the sins of the son were not visited on the father, who was later given the honour of escorting the future Queen, Anne of Cleves, to London.

Exterior, the back of the house, from the west.

The King showed his favour to Sir Richard by coming to stay as his guest in 1533. Four and a half centuries later the anniversary of that visit was honoured by another royal arrival, when the Prince and Princess of Wales came to open the spectacular Renaissance Exhibition at Sutton Place in 1983.

Richard Weston had travelled on the Continent and must also have admired Wolsey's great palace at Hampton Court so recently completed, for Sutton Place shows the marked influence of both experiences in its style, colouring and exterior decoration. He used the smaller traditional bricks with terracotta ornamentation of the Italian Renaissance style that are such an attractive feature of Hampton Court. One of the present Trustees, John Julius Norwich, brings the authority of his specialist knowledge of Italy to his enthusiasm for Sutton Place: 'I think that what makes Sutton really exciting is the fact that it's just about the first house to be built in England without any form of fortification or defence, no moat, no serious battlements, no watchtowers, nothing like that; up to the Wars of the Roses, really up to about 1500 nobody was safe enough in England to build a house like this. The terracotta decoration has come straight from Italy, and it's just about now in the 1520s when this house is being built that the first breath of the Italian Renaissance comes to England. All these little winged dancing cherubs, *putti* the Italians would call them, come from Italy and Sutton is only the second house in England that has them.'

The tiles set into the wall have Richard Weston's initials on them, and between them a little barrel or tun, a rebus which is the second half of his name – the West tun. Originally the house was built round a quadrangle but much later the north side with its four-storey gatehouse collapsed and in the eighteenth century was finally demolished, so that now it has more of the traditional Elizabethan E-shape. In 1571 Queen Elizabeth slept here, but a few days afterwards a fire broke out and did a lot of damage. After the high point of the Queen's visit, the family and the house gradually fell upon hard times. The Westons suffered like the Howards for their adherence to the Catholic faith, and although Sutton Place escaped the fate of Arundel Castle in the Civil War, the family found it increasingly difficult to maintain the house in good repair, and by the nineteenth century they were forced to let it.

Repairs were now badly needed, and under the tenancy of Frederick Harrison the first of a series of 'improvements' was embarked on. With the help of the great Victorian architect, Norman Shaw, he rebuilt the East Wing, which had remained a gutted roofless shell since the great fire of 1571, and fitted out the Long Gallery in place of the former chapel, which was not needed now that there was a church in the park. (The Long Gallery is now used for suppers after the concerts.)

Charles Alban Buckler designed the Victorian stained glass windows on the staircases, incorporating the coats of arms of all the families who had lived here. One of them was taken out recently, but the local Council and the Victorian Society are fighting a rearguard action against the Stanley Seeger trustees, who want to take out the second one to let in more light to the East Wing staircase. John Julius Norwich is particularly concerned about this. 'I don't think it's particularly beautiful. And we've got this marvellous garden which has never looked better in 500 years, but you can't see it.' He thinks the colours in the Victorian glass are 'clashy and raw', especially by comparison with the original stained glass windows that remain in the Great Hall. 'These are as old as the house, in some cases I think they are probably older. Quite a lot of them are fifteenth century, the very latest bits are perhaps the very early sixteenth. One marvellous picture shows a jester wading in a river to pick up a duck which somebody's shot, and an absolutely furious elephant underneath.'

The Brussels tapestries in the Great Hall and the Dining Room were brought here by Lord Northcliffe, the press baron who was the tenant from the turn of the century to 1917, and who spent millions to make the house suitable for his scale of entertaining. The Duke of Sutherland bought the estate from the Weston family in 1919, but the most famous of all its owners was J. Paul Getty, who bought it from the Duke in 1959, and lived here until his death in 1976. The tales of the meannesses of 'the richest man in the world' are legendary. The pay-phone he installed for the use of his guests has now been removed, but not the fibreglass ceilings and plywood panelling he put in. John Julius Norwich remembers visiting the miserable millionaire here, and says the atmosphere was 'suicidally gloomy. He lowered the ceilings and he certainly lowered my spirits'.

After his death the Getty Oil Corporation sold Sutton Place and another American multi-millionaire, Stanley J. Seeger, took a long lease of the house and parkland. In 1982 he transferred his lease to the Sutton Place Heritage Trust, and appointed a group of eminent Trustees to advise on the alterations and the programme of events. Sir Hugh Casson's firm of architects undertook the alterations in the house, and Sir Geoffrey Jellicoe was virtually given a blank cheque to landscape the gardens. In addition to them and Lord Norwich other Trustees and advisers include Henry Moore, Sir Peter Scott, Dame Margot Fonteyn, and Sir Roy Strong. Roger Chubb was brought in from Sotheby's as the Executive Trustee to administer the programme with a staff of 60, and in a phenomenally short time the house was transformed and the gardens were laid out.

Much of the redecoration has been done to set off the Seeger art collection to best advantage, estimated conservatively at around £25 million. Many walls have been painted white, others lined with corduroy, and the staircase panelling up to the Long Gallery is now a rather startling pink, grey and blue.

169

The Great Hall, with
16th Century Flemish
tapestry.

The Dining Room, with
Paul Getty's polystyrene
ceiling.

The Great Hall shows the typical contrasts to be seen in the house. At one end hangs a sixteenth century Flemish tapestry, at the other a Francis Bacon triptych – 'Studies of the Human Body', 1979 – in which a nearly nude man appears to have been tortured, and these disturbing images stand out starkly against an unsettlingly bright orange background.

Through the archway is what is now called the Bull Hall, from the large painting of a bull that dominates it. Painted by the nineteenth century artist John Glover, it is reminiscent of the famous life-size 'Bull' picture by the seventeenth century Dutch animal painter, Paulus Potter. It too is in sharp contrast to everything else in this Hall, which John Julius Norwich thinks is the secret of the effect. 'There's a sort of wild variety of everything all coming together. I think that's what makes Sutton such a fascinating place, you never quite know what's going to be round the next corner.'

Two great bronze torcheres stand each side of the Bull painting, opposite two antique Korean chairs with between them a pair of ancient stone carved consoles that look Assyrian, and in the corner an astronomical clock made by the English firm of Edward Cockey. 'It's an eighteenth century clock in a mad top-heavy case. It's got a 24-hour dial, and it tells you the day of the week and the date of the month, and the phase of the moon. I think if you really look very, very hard it can probably even tell you the time.'

John Julius Norwich pointing out the map of the world on the bull's hide. Painted by John Glover.

Up the staircase from the Bull Hall is the Great Chamber, which is now used for concerts and also doubles as the Library. Beyond it are the bedrooms which are extraordinary by any standards and must be unique in a house of this period, where only the Tudor Room has been decorated in the appropriate style. The Queen of Norway Room is named after the sixteenth century portrait hanging in it, but the contents of the rest of the bedroom are a deliberate mixture of other periods – a modern sofa, a Venetian streetlamp, and a French neo-classical bed whose white cover stands out in stark contrast to the black hessian walls. The Guard Room holds a huge Victorian dog basket bed, a Chippendale wardrobe, an eighteenth century Gothic fireplace, and an extraordinarily hideous hanging light made from twisted stag antlers that looks like a prop from a horror-movie.

Next door however is an equally striking example of good taste – the Liberty Room which is a perfect evocation of the pre-Raphaelite movement and its followers. The room is named after the famous store that supplied the furniture and furnishings, the art nouveau wall-hangings full of twining tendril shapes, and the marquetry work of animals in inlaid woods on the bed, washstand and chairs, of owls, swans and dolphins. And the room is not merely a show-case. As John Julius Norwich explains, 'If you're invited for the weekend that's probably where you'll be put!' There is a Tiffany lamp-shade, a period gramophone, and a Burne-Jones picture of a beautiful girl. If the soft feminine charms of this room are intended to offset the hard masculine character of the adjoining Guard Room, there is no doubt which is the more inviting place to sleep in.

The large Drawing Room and the other smaller rooms downstairs contain the rest of the Seeger collection of nineteenth and twentieth century art, and one of the expressed aims of the Trust is to support the work of contemporary artists. All this is part of what Roger Chubb sees as the exciting challenge of bringing an important country house back to life again. 'I find that so many English houses have in the last forty or fifty years become rather mummified without the driving force to be creative. Their lives seem almost to have stopped and the most exciting thing here has been making Sutton Place pull up its socks and start living again in the 1980s.'

One of the most living things is a garden, and one of Stanley Seeger's most inspired acts was to call on a man with a life-time's experience of garden design on a grand scale, and to give him virtually *carte blanche*. The only surviving founder-member of the Institute of Landscape Architects (created in 1929), Sir Geoffrey Jellicoe is recognised as the doyen of his profession. Naturally he was anxious about taking on such a large project in case he and Stanley Seeger did not see eye to eye. 'But the moment I met him I realised we were on the identical wavelength in ideas and those ideas are very simple. The landscape created today is still a continuum of what has happened in the

The Liberty Bedroom.

past so that we do something now which grows out of what has happened in the past and we hope that in the future it will, centuries to come, go on growing.'

In his youth Sir Geoffrey studied the great Italian gardens, and the fruits of that work were published in 1925 in *Italian Gardens of the Renaissance*, now long out of print and a collector's item. His more recent work *The Landscape of Man* reveals how much he is influenced by the great gardens of the past, although not as a restoration, more as 'a restoration of ideas'. He notes approvingly that Petrarch is said to have been the first Western man to climb a mountain for the sake of the view, and Sir Geoffrey too thinks on the grand scale.

173

He has created a lake to the north of the house and raised its level several feet above the River Wey, so that its surface is visible from the house. 'It is nearly half a mile long and has been moulded to take a Henry Moore sculpture on a colossal scale, which Stanley very much wanted to have there,' Sir Geoffrey explains. 'The shaping of that lake is as it were the beginning of creation, the soil is used to form a hill which is the male form, and the other end of the lake is the female form, and between them lies a little knoll on which the Henry Moore will be placed, and this is the beginning and birth of civilisation.' The lake has been fashioned in the shape of a fish to remind us that life began in water, but the whole effect can only be seen properly from the air.

The Paradise Garden.

The stepping-stones from the House to the Paradise Garden.

In his last book he cites the medieval ideal of 'a goodly gardeyn to walk ynne closed with high walls embattled', as depicted in the Paradise Garden of a Rhenish master of the fifteenth century, and at Sutton Place he has created a walled Paradise garden that draws on the inspiration not just of his Italian masters but also of the classical Greek and Persian originals too. You step straight out of the East Wing on to stepping stones across a large pool covered with great spreads of water-lilies. The lay-out is symbolic as well as attractive. 'In order to get to the Paradise Garden you must go through certain hazards, and the hazard out here is in fact the water and the stepping stones. You have to keep your eyes on the ground, and for the moment as you cross this you don't see the Paradise Garden, what you might see underneath the water is a special design.'

The curling paths add to the delicate sense of mystery. 'In a Paradise Garden you don't want to see the whole area at once, it wants to be inviting and attractive and you want to create the urge to explore.' The paths lead the visitor to the four fountains in the arbours, which are intended as places to sit and converse. The numbers are symbolic too. 'The Persian Paradise Garden was a symbol of Heaven brought to Earth and it was a square with the four rivers of Paradise flowing through it. The sound of water was the basic thing in the Persian Paradise garden because life depends on water.'

Wherever you walk in this garden there is the sound of water, not just from the gently splashing fountains, but gushing from the mouths of terra-cotta gargoyles set into the walls. So that these new walls should blend with the Tudor house Sir Geoffrey ordered 180,000 specially made narrow bricks, which at present are still recognisably new, but will mellow with age to match the tones of the house. The winding paths are paved with old bricks, and the plants have been allowed to overflow on to them to give the constant impression of walking through nature. The walls enclose some large mature trees at the end, where Sir Geoffrey is creating a wild Moss Garden as a contrast. At intervals in the walls are set grilled openings which offer glimpses of the wood outside. At night concealed lighting makes the whole enclosed area into the most romantic setting, and both the electric wiring and the many water-pipes have been buried out of sight to preserve the magical and artfully natural atmosphere.

Leaving the Paradise Garden to the south side takes the visitor through the rows of orange and lemon trees lining the path. A diversion left through the line of clipped yews leads to the top of an overgrown steep slope where the next plan is to construct an elaborate cascade (partly inspired by the Princess of Wales's wedding dress) with a grotto underneath the great fountain at its head. This is the only major construction not yet undertaken, but the plans are so ingenious that the Queen Mother is just one of the many visitors who have expressed a wish to return to see them completed.

Continuing the path along the south front, under the huge cedar, leads to the old walled garden which now surrounds the Miro Pool. Stanley Seeger asked Sir Geoffrey to convert the old swimming pool into something which could be enjoyable as a work of art in itself. 'And he gave me certain clues, similar things he'd seen in California like floating baskets of flowers, and I thought now how am I going to cope with this, but I knew he had an idea lurking behind him which he always has, and when I started sketching out I realised that one could have a raft which would be a biological shape. In order to get to the raft you have to have stepping stones, and those stepping stones in order to be free and easy and irrational without much meaning to them had to be rather difficult and illogically placed.' The circular stepping stones and the kidney shaped raft were certainly inspired by Miro, but their

The Ben Nicholson 'Wall'.

creator is quick to point out that a painter can change his creation with a stroke of the brush, whereas a landscape architect finds it much more difficult to change something if he makes a mistake.

While being inspired by Miro, Sir Geoffrey Jellicoe also passionately espouses the work of those two modern masters Henry Moore and Ben Nicholson, who for him are the two English figures of this century to have brought most to landscape design. Moore represents biological man, Nicholson geometrical man.

Their two great works at Sutton Place would have been out of both scale and period near the house, so their sites were chosen with care, to be studied and appreciated in lonely isolation, the Moore by the lake, while the huge

177

gleaming white Nicholson wall is only approached by a winding path through the woods. As you step out into the open the massive white marble piece is set against a dark green background of trees, and the long pool in front of it reflects the shapes within it.

Nicholson had nurtured his 'Project for a Wall' for many years, and for all his great friend Sir Geoffrey's efforts on his behalf it had not been brought to fruition until now. 'I admire his work so tremendously,' says Sir Geoffrey. 'I think he lifts you right out of the present into a great world of thought; and for eight years in half a dozen or more different places I've been designing a wall for him. Either the site was wrong or the materials weren't good enough, or the money wasn't there, or the client basically didn't like it. One public authority very nearly did, one even got a grant paid from the Arts Council, but it still couldn't be done because there still wasn't enough money to do a Nicholson Wall. It was a very expensive business because the materials would have to stand the tests of time.' At last there was a client who would not jib at the expense, which finally came to hundreds of thousands of pounds. Since there may well never be another one made it is fortunate that the breathtaking splendour of this one has found such a perfect setting.

But incongruity has also been deliberately planned in the gardens as it has in the house. Stanley Seeger's catholic taste embraced the surrealism of Magritte and the classical sculpture of ancient Rome, so this unlikely combination proved to be the solution for one problem posed by the client to his architect. 'Stanley Seeger had bought five splendid heroic vases from the Mentmore sale, and one of them had arrived here and the other four were sitting around somewhere waiting to be placed. I thought to myself, "Now how on earth am I going to cope with these vases?" And he said "I'd like them placed in this garden". The character of Sutton Place is English domestic, and these vases of ancient Rome were totally out of keeping, so I thought turning over his points about Magritte that his great quality was the juxtaposition of opposites, and that one could transform this idea into landscape.'

His solution was to take the great axis of the path along the south front which classically would have led to a Temple or other striking feature, but here ended at a tiny magnolia totally out of scale, and placed the five huge vases so that they appear to be doing homage to the little tree, framed through a window in the wall, in the surrealistic spirit of Magritte. The whole design of the total landscape at Sutton Place is an allegory of creation, life and aspiration. Sir Geoffrey intends the visitor to move from the domestic scene of the pleasure grounds to the Magritte garden which is designed as an introduction to the sublime and contemplative Nicholson Wall. He calls this 'topsy turvy surrealism'.

178

It does not matter to Sir Geoffrey whether visitors query the reasons why he has laid out the gardens as he has, he is more concerned with the effects on their subconscious, which is where he thinks we respond to nature, emotionally rather than intellectually. He also knows that neither he nor we will see his work at its best. Landscape architects design for posterity, and just as we admire the beauty of Capability Brown's eighteenth century vistas now, so it is future generations who will enjoy Sir Geoffrey's creations in their full maturity. For a man whose previous commissions have ranged from the garden of the young Duke of York, later King George VI, to the Communist Italian City of Modena, and the Royal Horticultural Society at Wisley, and whose legacies include the landscape at Chequers and the Kennedy

The Mentmore Vases in the Magritte Garden.

Memorial at Runnymede, it is particularly heartwarming that his last great commission in his eighties should have placed no financial restraints on his imagination, and called on the fruits of a lifetime's experience.

Sir Richard Weston built Sutton Place under the beneficial influence of the Italian Renaissance, four and a half centuries ago. Now the house has undergone a modern Renaissance, drawing on the New World as well as the old, in the bold spirit that was previously exercised only by the great owners of earlier centuries, and has so rarely been possible in our own.

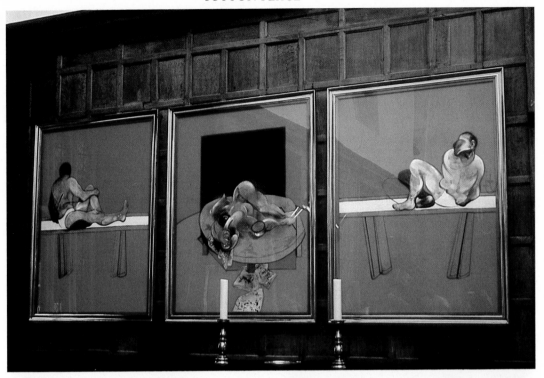

Top, page 171. *Studies of the Human Body*, by Francis Bacon, 1979. *Above left*, page 168. The Staircase to the Long Gallery, with Victorian stained glass windows. *Above right*, page 169. Detail of the stained glass in the Great Hall.

181

Page 176. The Mirò Pool, with raft and stepping-stones.

Top, page 197. Some of Churchill's paintings and his easel, in the studio at Chartwell. *Above left*, page 195. Winston Churchill in one of his wartime siren-suits, by Frank Salisbury. *Above right*, page 193. Clementine Churchill by Douglas Chandor, 1946.

Page 200. Sir Winston's favourite seat in the garden after his retirement.

CHARTWELL

WINSTON Churchill once wrote, 'A day away from Chartwell is a day wasted.' It was his home for the last 40 years of his life, and since his death it has belonged to the National Trust, which has preserved it as a living memorial to the man once simply described by the historian A. J. P. Taylor as 'the saviour of his country'. His presence still broods here, as strongly as that of the Duke of Wellington at Stratfield Saye, and draws thousands of visitors every year, many of them from abroad, who come to pay tribute to the memory of the man who led his country through its Darkest Hour.

For a man born in the splendour of Blenheim Palace the house seems remarkably modest, but he fell in love with the place the moment he saw it. He was drawn to it by its setting and its views across the Weald of Kent, rather than by the house itself, which in 1922 was an ugly Victorian mansion in a state of some disrepair. Its previous history was undistinguished and much of the building only dated from the middle of the nineteenth century, although the central core is much older. It was named after a clear spring, the Chart Well, which now runs into the upper lake of the chain that Churchill soon built.

He found the property near Westerham in Kent in the summer of 1921, and at first his wife was as enthusiastic about the prospect as he was. But she soon discovered the drawbacks were considerable. Not only was it built on the side of a hill so that the front was overshadowed by trees and thick rhododendrons, but much of the house was damp and rotten and needed substantially rebuilding. But for once in her life she could not sway him from his impulsive decision. He merely bided his time and in September 1922 took his three eldest children, Diana, Randolph, and Sarah, off on a mystery tour to the country while their mother was recovering from the birth of her youngest child, Mary.

He told the children he was only thinking of buying the place, but they were so thrilled by it that they pestered their father to buy it. Their excitement knew no bounds when he finally confessed that he had already bought it. But the enthusiasm of the four of them did not impress Clementine. Although the house and 80 acres of grounds only cost £5,000, she knew that it would cost far more to make it habitable. The bill for the transformation finally totalled another £18,000. This was not an inconsiderable sum for a man who for much of his life had to earn his living by his pen, and at the time he bought Chartwell Lloyd George's coalition government had just collapsed. At the ensuing election, he lost his seat in Dundee and, following an operation for appendicitis, he now found himself 'without an office, without a seat, without a party, and without an appendix'.

In 1921, however, he received a totally unexpected legacy, and two years later he published the first volume of his history of the First World War, *The World Crisis*, which together solved his immediate financial worries, and the following year he was both back in the House of Commons as M.P. for

Exterior from the south.

Epping and in the Government as Chancellor of the Exchequer. The two years out of Parliament he had put to good use supervising the changes at Chartwell. His architect was Philip Tilden who wrote much later 'No client that I have had ... has ever spent more time, trouble, or interest in the making of his home.' But the difficulty and expense of eradicating all the dry rot which proved to have taken such a hold in the house led to increasingly strained relations between owners and architect.

Tilden's main achievement was to turn the aspect of the house through 90°, so that all the main rooms could take advantage of the wonderful view to the south. This entailed building out a large four-storeyed wing, extending the frontage each side of the original house, and stripping out the later additions to reveal the old beamed ceilings, the best of which is to be seen in the study on the top floor.

The front of the house was simplified, and now looks very much of this century, apart from the early eighteenth century wooden doorway which was brought here during the alterations. Because of the steep slope behind, the front door leads into what is actually the second floor. A constant stream of guests and visitors of many kinds passed through this door in the period between the wars. In the twenties Churchill's official duties at the Exchequer kept him more in London, but his years in the political wilderness in the

The front of the House today, transformed by the architect, Philip Tilden.

187

Thirties made Chartwell the hub of his political and literary activity. His output was fantastic. Apart from writing over 200 articles for newspapers and magazines, he published *My Early Life*, *The Eastern Front*, *The Life of Marlborough* in four volumes, and wrote a large part of *The History of the English-Speaking Peoples*. He was not daunted by the demands of such massive subjects. 'Writing a long and substantial book is like having a friend and companion at your side, to whom you can always turn for comfort and amusement, and whose society becomes more attractive as a new and widening field of interest is lighted in the mind.'

He revelled in the use of language, whether it was on the platform or the page and once told the Authors' Club that 'no one could set himself to the writing of a page of English composition without feeling a real pleasure in the medium in which he worked, the flexibility and the profoundness of his noble mother tongue. The man who could not say what he had to say in good English could not have very much to say that was worth listening to at all'.

His phenomenal output of books, articles and speeches entailed long hours in his study, and much of it was dictated rather than written, while he paced up and down. Visitors for the weekend would hear his measured tread above them matched by the measured cadences of that famous voice. (It is no wonder that he was invariably late for his meals.) Lady Soames remembers

Left Lady Soames in her father's study, with his Despatch Box as Chancellor of the Exchequer. *Opposite* Lord Randolph Churchill at his desk, when Chancellor of the Exchequer, by Edwin Ward.

her father's study was 'sacred territory' in which the children seldom set foot. One of Churchill's pet hates was whistling, especially if he was working, and Lady Soames blames her poor whistling ability on this. 'I always say I'm a very bad whistler and have difficulty in whistling for my dogs because I wasn't allowed to practise as a child.'

A portrait of his father, Lord Randolph Churchill, hangs next to the fireplace. He is shown writing at his Treasury desk with a quill pen. Above it are framed the figures of his 1886 Budget, showing a total expenditure for Imperial Britain of £82 million, and a declared surplus. Father and son were both Chancellors of the Exchequer, and Winston's own black despatch box which he used then stands next to the picture. Mary Soames believes Churchill's warmth as a father owes much to his experience with his own father 'whom he greatly admired but with whom he never had a very close relationship, which my father always regretted. I think he always tried to make it up with his own children and particularly with Randolph'.

Hanging from the study rafters are three flags – the Union Jack that was flown in Rome on June 5, 1944, the first British flag to fly in a liberated Capital, and his two standards as Knight of the Garter and Lord Warden of the Cinque Ports. The desk itself now holds photographs of the family, miniatures of his parents, and busts of Napoleon and Nelson. The book-

shelves hold mostly historical volumes. Mary Soames' impression of him as a child, 'apart from his warm lovingness, was what a tremendous worker he was. The whole life at Chartwell really was round my father's working schedule, and though it's true he didn't usually get up very early in the morning, he used to work in bed from an early hour; then there were all his ploys outside, building walls, making rock gardens, then after we'd all gone to bed he would come up here and work into the early hours of the morning.'

He relished the satisfactions of manual labour as a contrast to his mental exertions, and he left enduring monuments to that effort in the gardens. He built most of the long wall round the three-acre kitchen garden with his own hands over a period of seven years, and became so proficient that he could lay a brick a minute. He even got his bricklayer's ticket, paying five shillings to the Amalgamated Union of Building Trade Workers as an 'adult apprentice', rather to the annoyance of his trade unionist critics. His enthusiasm for everything he touched was almost wearing. 'I have had a delightful month building a cottage and dictating a book: 200 bricks and 2,000 words a day.'

His lake-building was equally ambitious. He decided to construct three lakes to flow into each other, and called on his scientific adviser, Professor Lindemann, to calculate the water-flow. Lindemann solved this aesthetic problem with the same application and despatch he brought to the rather more testing scientific questions the Prime Minister put to him during the War.

But neither of them then could see that Churchill would eventually be entrusted with the nation's leadership, though his lonely voice warned of the coming conflict through the thirties. Others in positions of special knowledge in the Armed Forces and Civil Service risked their careers to keep him informed, and a growing stream of visitors made their way to Chartwell. Mary Soames was a teenager then, but remembers how the march of world events and her father's congenital distaste for social small-talk made mealtimes riveting occasions.

'Round the table were often gathered the few people who really understood with my father what dangers our country and all the free world were facing,' she says. 'I began to realise there was something doom-laden on the horizon, and I particularly remember my father recited a verse he'd seen in a newspaper about a railway accident which had occurred because the driver fell asleep:

> "And who is in charge of the clattering train?
> The carriages creak, and the couplings strain,
> And the pace is fast and the points are near,
> And sleep has deadened the driver's ear,
> And the signals flash through the night in vain,
> For death is in charge of the clattering train."

The lakes created by Churchill before the war.

Even now it sends a thrill down my spine but as a child I just gripped the arms of my chair, as it brought vividly home what my father and a few, only too few, people really saw, which was the approaching danger.'

Dinner was often a long meal and the talk sometimes went on late into the night. The plain oak table was made specially for the room by Heal's to a seventeenth century design, and the chairs were made to the host's very specific instructions:

'The Dining Room chair has certain very marked requisites. First, it should be comfortable and give support to the body when sitting up

191

straight; it should certainly have arms, which are an enormous comfort when sitting at meals. Second, it should be compact. One does not want the Dining Room chair spreading itself, or its legs, or its arms, as if it were a plant, but an essentially upright structure with the arms and the back almost perpendicularly over the legs. This enables the chairs to be put together if need be, which is often more sociable, while at the same time the arms prevent undue crowding and elbowing.'

The large French windows of the Dining Room give directly on to the gardens and Churchill always liked to sit where he could see the beautiful view. The room has been restored now to its original pre-war state; however, after the war the room was used as a cinema, with the screen taking the place of the table. 'My papa used to sit in the front row with his poodle on his lap and it was great fun. Then people used to come in from the farm and the garden to enjoy the films, and my mother used to find them too long and used to creep out in the middle and go to bed.'

A painting in the Dining Room by William Nicholson (a Silver Wedding present from their friends), shows the Churchills breakfasting at this table. Winston liked good plain food, preferred meat to fish, and liked good wines

The Dining Room.

to accompany it, especially champagne. His great friend F. E. Smith, later Lord Birkenhead, once joked, 'Winston your tastes are extremely simple: you are easily satisfied with the very best.' Mealtimes could be quite rowdy affairs as well, as Lady Soames remembers. 'My father had a wonderful repertoire of Edwardian music hall songs and Vesta Tilley's songs, and we all used to join in with those; and then suddenly he'd switch to something wonderful like "Mine eyes have seen the glory of the coming of the Lord" and we'd all sing "Glory Hallelujah" at the tops of our voices – very noisy meals there were at some times!'

As in many households of his class and generation it was the custom after dinner for the ladies to retire to the drawing room, a custom that Clementine would not allow Winston to abuse. 'My mother would take the ladies away and she'd always say "Now Winston don't be too long", and sometimes it would be an hour and a half. But she got her own back if he'd really been a long time talking to his cronies, when she'd sweep all the ladies off to bed, and they would come out and find a note on the mat saying "goodnight darling".' Occasionally too, if in her opinion her husband had overstepped the mark, Clementine was quite capable of rebuking him publicly. 'My mother could sort of boil over like a pan of milk on the stove, suddenly, and I've known her sweep out of this room and that was very awkward, because we never knew whether to sweep as well and it was sad if one hadn't finished one's pudding.'

The long Drawing Room is directly above the Dining Room and bears Clementine's stamp. She chose the eighteenth century tables, mirrors and chandeliers, and the comfortable modern sofas and armchairs. The card-table for bezique is now laid out as if someone has just left a game to go in to dinner. Near it is a striking crystal cockerel by Lalique, a gift to her from President de Gaulle after the war. He allowed her to rebuke him when she thought he overstepped the mark and spoke slightingly of the British, whereas the two proud men were never the most comfortable of allies. (Winston's well-known outburst – 'Of all the crosses I have to bear the Cross of Lorraine is the heaviest', is, according to his daughter, quite apocryphal.)

Near the door hangs a half-length portrait in oils of Clementine by Douglas Chandor. Painted in 1946 it captures a trademark of hers that her daughter remembers affectionately. 'At the beginning of the war she practically abandoned hats, but as she loved to be very immaculate and tidy, and sometimes her days took her from dawn till dusk everywhere from factories to harbours, to lunch with the Lord Mayor and so on, she took to tying her head up in a bandana rather like the girls at the factories did. She had them made in all sorts of materials and they really looked very pretty.'

Above the fireplace hangs a picture of Winston's famous grey racehorse, Colonist II, painted by Raoul Millais. Racing was an activity that he took up

Above The Drawing Room. *Left* The French cockerel in crystal by Lalique, a gift from President de Gaulle to Lady Churchill.

194

after the war, aided and abetted by his son-in-law Christopher Soames. Colonist II soon became a popular winner and his successes gave the post-war leader of the Opposition much pleasure. On one occasion when he was attacking the Labour Government's expenditure plans a member opposite shouted, 'Why don't you sell your horse?' The instantaneous response brought a roar of laughter from the House. 'Well, that at least is a piece of property which has increased its value since it came under my control. As a matter of fact, I was strongly tempted to sell the horse, but I am doing my best to fight against a profit motive.'

The Drawing Room was always a place for relaxation, but it was expected that guests would also have their own work to do while the master of the house was writing in his study, so the Library across the hall from the Drawing Room was set aside for the use of visitors. The desk today holds signed photographs of King George VI and Queen Elizabeth taken in 1941, and on one wall there is a likeness by Frank Salisbury of the wartime Prime Minister in one of his siren suits, smarter versions of the workmen's boiler suits he used to wear for his pre-war bricklaying sessions. Facing him now is a relief model set into the wall, of Port Arromanches in Normandy used for the D-Day landings, showing clearly how the artificial harbour worked. The books on the shelves are historical volumes that overflowed from the study upstairs, and foreign-language editions of many of Churchill's works.

The Library reminds the visitor of some of the high-water marks of his career, but it is important to remember the troughs of despair and depression he suffered as well, which even made him contemplate having to sell Chartwell. In 1936 he wrote to his wife saying 'no good offer should be refused, having regard to the fact that our children are almost all flown, and my life is probably in its closing decade'.

Four years later, on May 10th, 1940, he became Prime Minister at the time of the country's greatest peril. He wrote: 'As I went to bed at 3 a.m. I was conscious of a proud sense of relief. At last I had the authority to give directions over the whole scene. I felt as if I were walking with Destiny and that all my past life had been a preparation for this hour and for this trial.'

He was now 66, and astonished much younger men by the punishing hours he worked, and the resilience he showed when the war went badly, but once his wife expressed a fear that he would not long survive it. In her long and moving biography of her mother, Mary Soames recounts a conversation Clementine had with Diana Cooper in Marrakech in 1944. 'I never think of after the war. You see, I think Winston will die when it's over. He's 70 and I'm 60 and we're putting all we have into this war, and it will take all we have.'

She wanted him to retire when peace finally came and not seek re-election as a party leader, having been the national leader for the last five years. She

Above 'Colonist II' by Raoul Millais. Sir Winston's prizewinning horse, which he raced in partnership with his son-in-law, Christopher Soames. *Left* The relief model of the Mulberry Harbour at Arromanches, used for D-Day landings, in the Library.

196

had not anticipated the overwhelming Conservative defeat in the 1945 Election, but when the results came in she tried to comfort him by saying, 'It may be a blessing in disguise,' to which his wry response was, 'Well, at the moment it's certainly very well disguised.'

During the war neither of them had seen very much of Chartwell, as its lakes made it too much of an identifiable target for German bombers, and the prospect of an invasion through Kent made it impossibly vulnerable as a Prime Ministerial retreat. But still Churchill could not resist paying one or two flying visits in great secrecy during some of the darkest days of the war. After the war a group of their close friends bought it anonymously and presented it to the National Trust, on condition that Winston and Clementine should live there undisturbed during their lifetimes. At last they could enjoy its peace without the shadow of its cost hanging over them. So the second long span of their occupation began. Even when he returned to No. 10 Downing Street for the second time in 1951, Churchill endeavoured to spend as much time at Chartwell as at his official country retreat, Chequers. The house began to fill up with all the wartime memorabilia that can still be seen there today – cartoons, photographs, maps, uniforms, gifts and insignia of foreign orders. (He could be surprisingly vague about the protocol associated with the latter, for a man so used to uniforms and decorations. He once went to a reception in France wearing the *Medaille Militaire* in the wrong lapel, and every other man there sporting the same decoration transferred theirs from the left to the right lapel. When this gesture was later pointed out to him he said, 'The French are the best diplomats in the world.')

One facet of Churchill's temperament that cannot fail to strike the visitor to Chartwell is his lifelong regard for the Crown, and not just the person who currently wore it. His emotional defence of Edward VIII at the time of the Abdication caused one of the very few occasions when he virtually got howled down in the House of Commons, but his admiration for the brother who succeeded him was marked by his wreath at George VI's funeral in 1952 inscribed just with the two words 'For Valour', the citation of the Victoria Cross. He was Prime Minister at the time and thus became Queen Elizabeth II's first Prime Minister. Two photographs of her catch the eye at Chartwell, one on her way to open Parliament which Mary Soames says 'he always thought showed her in full and glorious flight', and one on the eve of his retirement as Prime Minister on the steps of No. 10, as she left his farewell dinner. The following day he left Downing Street for Chartwell, and said to a reporter who greeted him on the steps, 'It's always nice to come home.'

But the photographs are outnumbered by the profusion of his paintings. He took up his brush in 1915 after the disaster in the Dardanelles, and it became over the years a source of great pleasure to him and a relief from the cares of office. He once said, 'If it weren't for painting, I couldn't live; I

Queen Elizabeth II on her way to open Parliament. It hangs in the study, and was Churchill's favourite photograph of his Sovereign.

couldn't bear the strain of things.' He painted over 500 pictures, quite a number of which hang in the house, and many more in the Studio he had built in the garden. They are mostly landscapes and still-lifes, with just a few portraits, and although he acknowledged the help and advice of Walter Sickert he did not care for the latter's 'poor browns', preferring the bold and bright colours he found in the Mediterranean. In his essay, *Painting as a Pastime*, he wrote that if he ever got to Heaven he would like to spend the first million years painting so he could try to get to the bottom of the subject.

A few yards walk from the Studio is the walled garden that now contains the Golden Wedding present from the Churchill children to their parents – an avenue of golden roses, 146 standards and bushes in 29 varieties of gold and yellow. Since the Anniversary fell in September, and the roses would not bloom until the following June, Randolph asked a number of prominent British artists to paint a named rose each in a beautifully mounted vellum book, with the pages bordered with roses tooled in gold. The artists included Augustus John, Matthew Smith, Duncan Grant, Cecil Beaton, Paul Maze and his political colleague, R. A. Butler. The bookmark is a miniature blue Garter sash embroidered with the initials W.S.C.

and the motto of the Order 'Honi soit qui mal y pense' – a gift from the Garter King-of-Arms, Sir George Bellew. Today the Golden Book stands open at a different page each day on a side-table in the Dining Room, and the roses bloom all summer long sheltered by the great man's own wall.

The gifts and good wishes that poured in to celebrate his Golden Wedding in 1958, were followed by another avalanche of congratulations on his 90th birthday in 1964, but now the end was near. On January 11th, 1965 he had a stroke. When word got out that he was dying the whole world seemed to hold its breath. Press and television set up a 24-hour vigil, waiting for the end, which finally came on January 24th.

In death, as so often in life, he continued to hold centre-stage. The Queen

The Golden Rose Garden, the gift of the Churchill children for their parents' Golden Wedding in 1958. Beech hedges flank the rose walk.

had told the then Prime Minister, Harold Macmillan, seven years earlier that when Churchill died she wished him to have a Lying-in-State and a State Funeral, an honour not given to a commoner since the Duke of Wellington.

After lying in state in Westminster Hall for three days, on Saturday, January 30th the coffin was taken through vast silent crowds to St Paul's Cathedral. The procession took an hour on a bitterly cold day. The Queen broke with custom and precedence in attending the funeral, and awaited the arrival of her father's great war leader and her own first Prime Minister, accompanied by his mourning family. Heads of State and Governments waited with her in St Paul's, and television cameras relayed the occasion around the world. After the service the coffin was taken by launch from Tower Pier to Waterloo as huge cranes dipped in salute and R.A.F. Lightnings flew past in formation. The last leg of the journey was by train to Long Handborough, near Bladon in Oxfordshire, where he was to be buried. He had originally wished to lie at Chartwell, but later changed his mind, and so his last resting-place is within sight of Blenheim where he was born, in Bladon churchyard with his parents and brother Jack.

Lady Churchill never lived at Chartwell again. She asked the National Trust to take it over immediately, and to restore it to its pre-war layout, so that the public should see the house as they had lived in it when her husband was at the height of his powers, and their children were growing up. She gave the Trust most of the contents – furnishings and memorabilia – that make Chartwell still look lived-in today, and make it so evocative of those eventful years when Winston warned of the Gathering Storm, until the call finally came to lead his country.

He once said, 'History with its flickering lamp stumbles along the trail of the past.' But the lamp burns steadily and brightly at Chartwell, which is filled with the evidence of Winston Churchill's historic wartime leadership, and this is what most of the thousands of visitors who come here from home and abroad expect to find. For Mary Soames, 'the Chartwell child', the place has more private resonances. It was her father's great delight to sit by the pool he had created and feed the fish, the golden orfe, with which he had stocked it. His chair is still placed in his favourite spot. 'He used to sit in that chair and in the box at the side were lovely consignments of fresh grubs for the fish, which they loved. And they used to come streaming across the pool when they saw his figure there. And then after he'd fed them he nearly always stayed for quite a long time in that chair in deep contemplation ... and I must say of all the places at Chartwell, this always evokes most strongly for me the presence and memory of my father.'

ACKNOWLEDGEMENTS

I have to thank first all those who so warmly welcomed our cameras into their homes to make the television series *An Englishman's Home* on which this book is based, and who so cheerfully and patiently put up with the demands we made on their time, their knowledge, their stamina, and their good nature: The Duke of Richmond and Lord and Lady March, Lord and Lady Romsey, The Duke of Norfolk, Sir Westrow and Lady Hulse, Edward and Verity Hulse, The Duke and Duchess of Wellington, Lord and Lady De L'Isle, The Earl of Pembroke, John Eyre, John Julius Norwich, Sir Geoffrey Jellicoe, and Lady Soames.

Secondly I must thank all their Administrators and Comptrollers who eased our path and pointed us in the right directions: David Legg-Willis, Bob Pullin, Roland Puttock, Norma Gilbert, Brian Bush, Douglas Messenger, Veronica Quarm, Roger Chubb, and Sheila Broome.

Thirdly I would like to thank all those at TVS who laboured to make the television series such a success: Jill Cochrane who presented it, Bob Gardam, Pat Phillips, Richard Argent, and Slim McDonnell who directed it, Jean Orba and Jane Reeve who researched it, and all the location and post-production crews who gave their skills and enthusiasm so unstintingly, and who I regret are too numerous to mention individually here, but who all know how much I owe them.

Two people who have put much time and painstaking effort into this book are Jill Young who typed, and retyped it, and Tony Nutley who took all the magnificent photographs which illustrate it.

I am grateful to my publishers, Nicholas and Suzanne Battle, who asked me to write it, and who so enthusiastically encouraged me throughout its creation.

Finally, I must thank my wife, Aileen, for sustaining me through those long weeks, and for being so understanding when my preoccupation with the past made me sometimes forget the needs of the present.

INDEX